SIDRAH STORIES

⫸ ⫷

A Torah Companion

STEVEN M. ROSMAN

UAHC Press

New York, New York

Adaptations credited to the Talmud throughout this book are from the
Talmud Bavli, the Babylonian Talmud, unless otherwise indicated.

To Bari,
for her love which inspires
and sustains me;
for her support which ever encourages
and nurtures me

To Aron,
for his friendship, his insightful ideas,
and his confidence

Library of Congress Cataloging-in-Publication Data

Rosman, Steven M.
  Sidrah stories: a Torah companion/Steven M. Rosman.
    p. cm.
  Summary: A collection of Jewish stories, including original tales and adaptations
from the Midrash, the Talmud, and the Chasidic masters, based on the weekly portions
from the Torah.
  ISBN 0-8074-0429-2
  1. Legends, Jewish—Juvenile literature. 2. Bible. O.T.
Pentateuch—Legends—Juvenile literature. [1. Folklore, Jewish.]
I. Title.
BM530.R68 1989
296.1'9—dc19   88-39869
                                                                            CIP
                                                                            AC

· CONTENTS ·

· INTRODUCTION ·

We Jews have been telling stories for a long time. Jotham told fables to the citizens of Shechem (Judges 9:8–15); Hillel told stories to his pupils (*Soferim* 16:7). Stories permeate the midrashic literature. They are found in the secret tomes of the mystics. *Badchanim,* the medieval Jewish jesters, spun tales at weddings and other celebrations. Chasidim told parables to teach Torah and electrify the souls of their disciples. We have written fairy tales, folktales, tales of morality, and tales of intrigue. We have our own versions of Cinderella and Aesop's fables. Sometimes we have adapted material of the cultural milieu, and sometimes we have created lore out of whole cloth.

The stories in this book perpetuate this wonderful legacy. Some are adaptations of marvelous lore from the Midrash, the Talmud, or the chasidic masters. Some are original. All have in common a particular focus derived from the weekly *sidrah*. Ultimately, this is a book to engage the intermediate age student in the study of Torah. So, its stories grow from a verse or two from the *sidrah,* chosen because they provide a fruitful focus of encounter for the student of this age.

Despite the setting, these stories are meant to be told. Each is preceded by the verse or verses from the *sidrah* upon which its main idea is based. Each is followed with a discussion meant for the story-teller, which delineates some of the issues implied by the biblical verse, and by a series of questions, offered only as a catalyst to your own. Questions arise out of the storytelling event. So, trust that, at the story's conclusion, your telling will lead you to ask your listeners your own questions. Perhaps, your listeners will have some for you. Such is one of the joys of storytelling.

· BERESHIT ·

—»» ««—

A Most Precious Gift

AFTER ADAM AND EVE had eaten the forbidden fruit from the Tree of Knowledge of good and evil, God banished them from the Garden of Eden forever. As they walked through the eastern gate, they noticed a cherub whom God had stationed there as a guard. The cherub was to make sure that no one ever entered Eden again.

As they passed the cherub, Adam paused and turned to him. "Is there nothing we can do?" he asked. The cherub was silent. "Please tell us what we can do. We know nowhere else but Eden and we shall be lost without our home." Silence. The cherub did not move and did not answer.

Feeling all alone and so very sad, Adam and Eve walked back to the gate which was ablaze with fire and gazed for the last time at Eden.

The sun was beginning to set and the sky was full of purple and crimson and violet and orange. This was the world's first sunset. It was growing a bit colder—or so it seemed to Adam and Eve. Evening was coming and Adam and Eve had never seen evening before.

They embraced each other for they were frightened. It was at this moment that the heavens opened and a brilliant, blinding light shown through the parted sky.

It was God. Then, Adam and Eve heard God's voice. They had heard it often in Eden. God had taken walks with them and had shown them all the animals and all the different plants, trees, and flowers.

"See these beautiful creations," God had said to them. "They are for you to name and for you to care for. Enjoy My garden and enjoy the life I have given you. But do not eat from the fruit of the Tree of Knowledge of good and evil. It stands by itself in the midst of the garden. Beware that tree and heed My warning."

But Adam and Eve had disobeyed. They had eaten from the forbidden tree. Now God was calling to them again.

"My children. I have banished you from Eden and know that you are afraid. Even though I have punished you for your disobedience, I will always love you and seek to care for you. So, I will give you a special gift. It will relieve the sadness you feel and ease your anguish."

Suddenly, the light withdrew and the heavens closed. The sky was again filled with all the colors of sunset. Adam and Eve hugged each other and began to cry. Tears rolled down their cheeks and they tasted the salty flavor in their mouths. When they finally stopped crying, they felt better. Their sadness was gone and their hearts seemed lighter.

"This must be God's gift," said Eve. She lifted her hand to wipe Adam's face.

And so it is that this gift from God has been passed from Adam and Eve to us. Whenever we are troubled and sad, tears will flow from our eyes and comfort us. Truly, this is a very precious gift that God has given to us.

(Adapted from the Midrash)

After Adam and Eve were banished from Eden for eating the forbidden fruit, they faced life outside of paradise for the first time. This meant not only that they recognized their nakedness but, as the Torah tells us, they would have to toil for sustenance and endure the pain associated with childbirth. Adam and Eve were truly alone, facing a human mortality they had never known before. The poet John Milton referred to this devastating episode in human history in his epic, *Paradise Lost*. Ever since, when writers have wished to depict the notion of paradise, they have needed to resort to one word only, Eden. Moreover, *Gan-Eden*, the Garden of Eden, was used by the rabbis as a projection of the state of being to which humankind will return in the Messianic Age. Maybe, if the rabbis are right, humankind has Eden to look forward to, but Adam and Eve had to accept that they had left Eden behind them forever.

How do you think Adam and Eve felt when they walked out of the Garden of Eden? When was the last time you were really afraid? What frightened you? What did you do to make your fear go away? What was the gift God gave to Adam and Eve? How was it supposed to help them? A folk saying tells us: "When you pour your heart out (in tears), it feels lighter." Do you think that is true? Do you think Adam and Eve felt better after they cried? What do you think they did that first night outside of Eden?

At the end of forty days, Noah opened the window of the ark that he had made and sent out the raven; it went to and fro until the waters had dried up from the earth. Then he sent out the dove to see whether the waters had decreased from the surface of the ground.   Genesis 8:6–8

➤➤➤ ⧫⧫⧫

Why Noah Chose the Dove

WHEN THE PEOPLE sinned and God decided to punish them by sending the Flood, all the animals gathered around Noah's ark. Noah was a righteous man, and God had told him how to save himself and his family by building an ark that would float and shelter them when the waters rose.

The animals had heard a rumor that Noah was to take with him on the ark only the best of all the living creatures. So the animals came and vied with one another, each boasting about its own virtues and whenever possible belittling the merits of others.

The lion roared: "I am the strongest of all the beasts, and I surely must be saved."

The elephant blared: "I am the largest. I have the longest trunk, the biggest ears, and the heaviest feet."

"To be big and heavy is not so important," yapped the fox. "I, the fox, am the cleverest of all."

"What about me?" brayed the donkey. "I thought I was the cleverest."

"It seems anyone can be clever," yipped the skunk. "I smell the best of all the animals. My perfume is famous."

"All of you scramble over the earth, but I'm the only one that can climb trees," shrieked the monkey.

"The only one!" growled the bear. "What do you think I do?"

"And how about me?" chattered the squirrel indignantly.

"I belong to the tiger family," purred the cat.

"I'm the cousin of the elephant," squeaked the mouse.

"I'm just as strong as the lion," snarled the tiger. "And I have the most beautiful fur."

"My spots are more admired than your stripes," the leopard spat back.

"I am man's closest friend," yelped the dog.

"You're no friend. You're just a fawning flatterer," bayed the wolf. "I am proud. I'm a lone wolf and flatter no one."

"Baa!" blatted the sheep. "That's why you're always hungry. Give nothing, get nothing. I give man my wool, and he takes care of me."

"You give man wool, but I give him sweet honey," droned the bee. "Besides, I have venom to protect me from my enemies."

"What is your venom compared with mine?" rattled the snake. "And I am closer to Mother Earth than any of you."

"Not as close as I am," protested the earthworm, sticking its head out of the ground.

"I lay eggs," clucked the hen.

"I give milk," mooed the cow.

"I help man plow the earth," bellowed the ox.

"I carry man," neighed the horse. "And I have the largest eyes of all of you."

"You have the largest eyes, but you have only two, while I have many," the housefly buzzed right into the horse's ear.

"Compared with me, you're all midgets." The giraffe's words came from a distance as he nibbled the leaves off the top of a tree.

"I'm almost as tall as you are," chortled the camel. "And I can travel in the desert for days without food or water."

"You two are tall, but I'm fat," snorted the hippopotamus. "And I'm pretty sure that my mouth is bigger than anybody's."

"Don't be so sure," snapped the crocodile—and yawned.

5

"I can speak like a human," squawked the parrot.

"You don't really speak—you just imitate," the rooster crowed. "I know only one word, 'cock-a-doodle-doo,' but it is my own."

"I see with my ears; I fly by hearing," piped the bat.

"I sing with my wing," chirped the cricket.

There were many more creatures who were eager to praise themselves. But Noah had noticed that the dove was perched alone on a branch and did not try to speak and compete with the other animals.

"Why are you silent?" Noah asked the dove. "Don't you have anything to boast about?"

"I don't think of myself as better or wiser or more attractive than the other animals," cooed the dove. "Each one of us has something the other doesn't have, given us by God who created us all."

"The dove is right," Noah said. "There is no need to boast and compete with one another. God has ordered me to take creatures of all kinds into the ark, cattle and beast, bird and insect."

The animals were overjoyed when they heard these words, and all their grudges were forgotten.

Before Noah opened the door of the ark, he said, "I love all of you, but, because the dove remained modest and silent while the rest of you bragged and argued, I choose it to be my messenger."

Noah kept his word. When the rains stopped, he sent the dove to fly over the world and bring back news of how things were. At last she returned with an olive leaf in her beak, and Noah knew that the waters had receded. When the land finally became dry, Noah and his family and all the animals left the ark.

After the Flood, God promised that never again would he destroy the earth because of man's sins, and that seed time and harvest, cold and heat, summer and winter, day and night would never cease.

The truth is that there are in the world more doves than there are tigers, leopards, wolves, vultures, and other ferocious beasts. The dove lives happily without fighting. It is the bird of peace.

(Story by Isaac Bashevis Singer, reprinted by permission of Farrar, Straus, and Giroux)

Many flood stories were told by the ancient peoples of the Near East, among them, the epics of "Atrahasis" and "Gilgamesh" from Mesopotamia. The narrative we have come to call Noah differs from these versions in a number of important ways. Whereas the other epics depict a mortal very much at the mercy of capricious gods, our Torah presents Noah as a righteous person among his people, whose morality is the reason he is spared the fate of his brethren. The biblical account stresses living in accordance with God in a relationship governed by a *berit,* a covenant.

The story by Isaac Bashevis Singer describes Noah's first encounter with the animals that are to share the ark with him and his family. We all know that Noah sent a dove to search out dry land after the rain had subsided. In his story, Singer speculates about Noah's choice of the dove for this assignment. Why was it not the donkey, the lion, or the elephant that received this honor? Like the narrative upon which it is based, Singer has created a tale of moral significance and implication.

What are some of the animals Noah took into his ark? What kinds of boasts did they make? Why didn't the dove boast about itself the way all the other animals boasted about themselves? Why did Noah choose the dove to be his messenger? Are you more like the dove or the other animals when it comes to boasting? What can we learn from the dove?

The Lord said to Abram, "Go forth from your native land and from your father's house." Genesis 12:1

→》》 《《←

Abraham, the Idol Smasher

Terach, Abraham's father was an idol maker. Abraham used to sit in his father's workshop and watch as his father took heaps of clay and shaped them into animals of all kinds, creatures which had the heads of birds and the bodies of people, or mean-looking warriors. Then his father would bring these statues outside into his shop and sell them to people as gods. Terach, the idol maker, had gods for the home and gods for travel; he had gods for the farmers and gods for the merchants. He had gods of all kinds for all places and for all problems.

One day, Terach had to deliver a bag of idols to a man who lived far away.

"Abraham," said Terach, "you must watch the shop while I am gone. Just give people whatever they ask for."

And with that, Terach packed up a bag full of the clay statues he had made and left the shop.

Abraham was alone in the shop. He looked at the statues that filled his father's shelves. He could not believe that these strange and sometimes funny-looking clay figures could actually be gods. After all, his father was just a man. How could a man make a god?

Abraham was puzzled. He was so deep in thought that he did not notice that someone had entered the shop.

"Where is Terach?" cried the man. "Where is Terach?"

"I am Abraham, son of Terach," said Abraham. "Can I help you?"

"I have such problems with my business. I need a special idol to bring me a change of fortune."

So Abraham went to the shelves his father had filled with special idols meant to bring their owners good business. He picked one up. It was truly ugly. It had the head of an eagle, the body of a man, and the legs of a horse.

"Here you are," said Abraham, handing it over to the man. "It is guaranteed to bring you good business."

The man took it greedily from Abraham's grasp and looked it over from top to bottom. It must have pleased him because he reached into a small bag he carried around his neck, took out a couple of coins, and tossed them onto the counter. Then he hurried out of the shop.

All day long people came in and out of Terach's shop. One woman wanted an idol for her daughter to help her get married. Another woman wanted an idol that would keep her young and beautiful. Then there was a bald man who wanted an idol that would put hair back on his head.

Abraham brought each person exactly what had been requested. He simply went over to the shelves and looked for the sections which held the idols he sought. One section was labeled "marriage-makers," another was labeled "beauty-makers," and another was labeled "hair-makers."

After the last customer had left the shop, Abraham sat and wondered. "Don't these people know that my father made the clay statues with his own hands, right there in the back of the shop?" Then he stood up and shouted, "A man cannot make a god! God has created us and the whole universe we live in."

He was so angry that he picked up the broom he was supposed to use to sweep the floor and began smashing all the statues on all the shelves. He did not stop until the figures lay in bits and pieces on the shelves. That is, all the figures but one. Then he took the broom and placed it in the hands of the one remaining statue.

When Terach returned from his trip, he walked into the shop and was horrified to see the disaster which had befallen his idols.

"What happened? What calamity has struck the shop of Terach, the idol maker?"

"Father," said Abraham, "it was truly terrible. First, one of the idols turned to another, claiming it was the most powerful. Then, that other idol boasted that it was the most powerful. Then, before I could do anything, each one was shouting that it was the most powerful. And that is when it happened."

"That is when what happened?" asked Terach in a state of shock.

"That is when this large idol picked up the broom and cried, 'We shall see who is the most powerful!' And he began smashing the others to bits."

"That's impossible," screamed Terach. "I have made them all with my own hands. They are clay."

"I know they are only clay," said Abraham. "The true God cannot be the creation of us who are human. God is the Creator. We are the created."

With that Abraham left his father's shop and started out on the journey that made him the first Hebrew and the true patriarch of our people.

(Adapted from the Midrash)

The first words of the Torah portion have been translated in different ways: *"Lech-Lecha"* has been understood by some to mean "go forth"; others have translated it "go to yourself," implying an inner exploration of one's deepest beliefs. It is entirely possible to see our verse as meaning both. Before Abraham could go forth toward the land "that I [God] will show you," he had to delve deeply into himself and examine the very roots of his convictions. Did he have what it took to leave the security of his home and family? Our story is based upon the midrashic tale in which Abraham, then Abram, realizes that his family's fundamental faith in idolatry does not satisfy him. Ultimately, this young man rejects one of the basic ordering principles of his culture and embraces a theology which was to make him the "father of our people." With this in mind, perhaps, it is fair to suggest that Abram's first ordeal was not to "go forth" alone into the world; it was, rather, to make the introspective journey to the heart of his beliefs.

How old do you think Abraham was in our story? Give some reasons for your answer? What are Abraham's reasons for rejecting his father's belief in idols? If you were Abraham, what would you have told Terach when he returned to his store and found all the broken idols? Do you think it was difficult for Abraham to stand up to his father? Make up another ending to this story, describing what happened to Abraham after he left his father's shop.

· VAYERA ·

Looking up, he saw three men standing near him. As soon as he saw them, he ran from the entrance of the tent to greet them.   Genesis 18:2

→» «←

Reb Nissim and the Stranger

Rᴇʙ Nɪssɪᴍ was a *lamed-vavnik,* one of the thirty-six righteous individuals whose good deeds keep God from destroying this world when humankind becomes really evil. You might think that, if people as good as this truly existed, they would be famous. Not so. No one knows who these *lamed-vavnik*s are; their identities remain secret forever. It's possible that you yourself could be a *lamed-vavnik.* Only time will tell. Often, these religious people don't seem to be the ones whose good deeds had the power to save the world. They might be the poorest of all townspeople, even the least learned.

Reb Nissim was a *lamed-vavnik.* He seemed like a poor milkman to everyone who knew him. Each morning, before dawn, he would ride his horse–drawn cart to the homes of all the people of Kutsk. More often than not, his horse was too sick to pull alone and Reb Nissim would pull along with him.

This winter was the harshest anyone in Kutsk could remember. Many of the animals had perished from the cold or lack of food, or both. It was so cold that Reb Nissim's only cow did not give milk for weeks. With no milk there was no money. It was hard for Reb Nissim and his family. That first week after the cow stopped giving milk, there were still enough scraps of potatoes and bread to make a meal. There were even enough leftovers to prepare a meal for Shabbat. The next week, life was a bit more difficult. By the third week, the family was truly suffering. No one in Kutsk could help because they, too, had nothing. The winter seemed endless and the whole world looked bleak.

Still, Reb Nissim would say, "When does a Jew sing best? When he is hungry!" So, he would go about town with a *niggun* on his lips and the sound of Reb Nissim walking along made those who heard him feel better. You can't hear the grumble of an empty belly when you hum a *niggun*. Try it. If you can't hear the grumble, maybe you are not really hungry.

One day on his way home, Reb Nissim came upon a stranger dressed in beggar's garb. He leaned on a wooden stick as he walked slowly along the side of the road.

"Shalom Aleichem," called out Reb Nissim and he continued to hum his *niggun*.

"Aleichem Shalom," replied the stranger. "Do you know anywhere that I might be able to find some shelter from the biting wind and even, perhaps, something to eat?"

"Ah, my poor friend," said Reb Nissim. "Your misfortune is more than you know. You have wandered into the town of Kutsk where there is an abundance of snow and suffering but very little of anything else. Still, it is said, 'Let your home be wide open and the needy be members of your household.' So, nu, come home with me. Certainly, it is warmer in my home than on the street and, certainly, a scrap of food is better than none at all."

So Reb Nissim brought the stranger home with him. That night there was no feast in Reb Nissim's home, but there was singing and there was the warmth of friendship. Reb Nissim and the stranger exchanged stories all night long, to the delight of Reb Nissim's children.

Early the next morning, Reb Nissim got out of bed and prepared to go out to the barn to see if this was the morning, "May Messiah come!," when his cow would finally give milk once again. As he made his way past the stove toward the door, he noticed that the stranger was gone. There was no sign of him anywhere.

This was odd. "Why would he leave without saying good-bye," he wondered.

But what did Reb Nissim find when he entered the barn? Pails and pails everywhere he looked. Some were filled to the brim with rich white milk. The others, Reb Nissim could not believe his eyes. The pails not filled with milk were filled to the brim with silver and gold coins, which gleamed in the early morning light.

Reb Nissim rubbed his eyes to awaken from his dream. But, when he opened his eyes again, he discoverd that the pails were still there. This was no dream! It was a miracle.

"Is it not said," thought Reb Nissim, "that 'when a man has *mazal*, even his ox has calves!' So, why can't a cow have coins!" Reb Nissim smiled and chuckled at the thought.

Indeed, for a *lamed-vavnik*, nothing seems impossible.

(*Based on a folk saying, "He who has fed a stranger
may have fed an angel"*)

The verse from Genesis presents the motif of hospitality. Rabbinic tradition depicts Abraham as the chief exemplar of this mitzvah. One midrashic account explains that Abraham was sitting at the door of his tent so that he could watch out for strangers who might be passing by. Another says that Abraham asked one of his servants to take part in the preparations for his guests (18:7) in order to teach him about the mitzvah of *hachnasat orechim,* greeting guests. In our story, Reb Nissim follows in the footsteps of Abraham and welcomes an unusual stranger to his home.

Reb Nissim was a *lamed-vavnik*. What would a modern *lamed-vavnik* be like? What kinds of things would such a person do? Who do you think the stranger was? Are there people in our communities who have no place to live and no food to eat? What do we do for those people? What else can you do for them? Have you ever done anything to make a stranger feel welcome?

· CHAYE SARAH ·

Sarah's lifetime . . . came to one hundred and twenty-seven years. Sarah died in Kiriath-arba, now Hebron—in the land of Canaan.   Genesis 23:1–2

→》》 《《←

Goobi the Grub

Do you know what grubs are? You've seen them when you went to some old pond and walked among the high grass by the water's edge. There, see them, at ground level, sliding in and around the blades of grass! You might say that they are ugly. Fat, slippery, and wormlike, they dig around in the mud. To us, that kind of life may not sound like fun. But, those grubs you see down there are very happy. They love the feel of the cool, smooth soil and the warm security of their pond. When it is sunny, they can bask in the warmth or cool themselves in their damp surroundings. When it rains, they have even more mud to play in or they can dive under the water and listen as the raindrops pelt the pond's surface like the taps you might make when you play your drums.

So, you see, these grubs are very happy creatures. There is, however, one troubling mystery that has never been solved: When grubs reach a certain age they disappear, vanish, and are nowhere to be found. One day they are playing in the mud like everyone else and the next day they are gone, without telling anyone they were going away—no notes, no letters, nothing.

Well, Goobi, one young grub, was very curious about all this. He made a promise that, when he got older, he would leave a note before he disappeared and, then, he would come back to visit his friends by the pond and tell them where he had gone.

So, Goobi called all his friends over and told them his promise. Then, he balanced himself on the tail of his wormlike body until he stood up as straight and tall as he could. He dug his tail deep into the mud and spun himself around three times. That is how grubs make promises. His friends felt better because they thought that finally someone was going to solve the mystery.

A long time passed. Goobi and his friends continued to have fun in their pond playground. Still, older grubs disappeared and no one knew where they went.

One day, Goobi felt very strange. Something inside him was pushing him to slither over to one of the large reedlike plants along the water's edge. Slowly, he climbed up the plant. He did not know why he was climbing, but he knew that he had to. Finally, he reached the top of the reed and a weird feeling shook his body. Then, before he knew what was happening, a sticky fluid began oozing out from him. Automatically, instinctively, he began spinning the ooze around his body until he was completely surrounded by it. The ooze encased him like a second skin and he felt warm and safe inside. Somehow, he knew this was right.

Days passed. Goobi could not keep count of how many. He slept most of the time. Then, one day, suddenly, an alarm went off inside his head. Again, instinctively he began to dig himself out of his protective shell. The air felt very good. The sunshine was very bright and he had to squint in order to see.

As he squeezed his body out of his shell, he realized that something was very different. His body felt strange. It was hard to get out of his little shell, and he had to push, push, and push, and . . . uh, oh! He pushed so hard he fell out. Falling through the air, Goobi was scared. He was falling faster and faster and the ground was getting closer.

Then, a miracle occurred. Goobi stopped falling. In fact, he started rising in the air. He was flying. He looked at his sides, and there were two beautiful wings. He could not believe that these wings were attached to his body. But they were. Flying was easy and fun. Maybe even more fun than playing in the mud by the pond.

Speaking of the pond, there it was far below him. He could see the clouds and the blue sky reflected by the water's surface. And then he saw this strange creature with a shiny black body and wonderful wings.

"Who is that beautiful creature?" he asked himself. So, he looked around and around. "I don't see anyone," he said. "The only one flying above the pond is me. Me! Me! It can't be!"

But it was. Goobi the grub had become Goobi the beetle. He did not look like a grub anymore and he did not sound like one either. His voice was different.

When he flew over to where his grub friends were playing in the mud, no one recognized him. No matter how much he screamed, no one understood what he was saying.

"It's me, it's me, Goobi! Can't you hear me? I have come back to keep my promise. I know where all our friends disappeared to and what happened to them. Can't anyone hear me?"

But no one heard him. So, Goobi flew away to join his new friends. And, back at the pond, Goobi's grub friends wondered what had happened to him and if he was ever going to come back and keep his promise.

Goobi never went back to the pond again. "What's the point," he thought. "No one there knows me anymore."

So, Goobi spent his time playing with his beetle friends and he waited. "Someday my grub friends will become beetles like me and we can be friends again," said Goobi. That thought made him smile.

(*Adapted from a poem, "A Parable of Some Grubs," by Walter Dudley Cavert*)

The Kotzker Rebbe once said: "Death is merely moving—from one home to another: and, if we are wise, we will make the latter the more beautiful." Contrary to what many of us might think, the concept of an afterlife has been an essential Jewish belief since the days of the Mishnah. Maimonides even counted it among his thirteen basic truths. Yet, despite the overwhelming conviction in an afterlife, there has been a variety of opinions about its descriptions. Some have conceived the *olam haba,* the "world to come," as another Eden; others have imagined it to be more like a heavenly yeshivah.

Young children have great difficulty understanding the finality of death. As they grow up, they begin to paint their own picture of what happens after we die. This story is a parable about immortality. It could be used as the basis for a discussion on death and afterlife.

What happens to Goobi? Why can't his friends recognize him after he has become a beetle? What do you think is the meaning of the story? What does this story have to say about death? Do you agree or disagree with its message? Judaism teaches such things about death as: "Death is merely moving from one home to another"; "There is a time for everything under heaven—a time to be born and a time to die." Make up some sayings of your own by completing one of these sentences: (1) Death is like—; (2) After you die—; (3) The world to come is like —.

Rebekah conceived. But the children struggled in her womb.
. . . The first one emerged red, like a hairy mantle all
over; so they named him Esau. Then his brother emerged,
holding on to the heel of Esau; so they named him Jacob.

Genesis 25:21–22, 25–26

-》》 《《-

A Tale of Two Brothers

MANY, MANY YEARS AGO, in the land of Israel, there lived two brothers. Judah lived with his wife and children on one side of a large hill; Isaac lived alone on the other side.

Each brother planted fields of wheat, barley, and oats. At the time of the harvest each would gather his grain and store it for the winter. Year after year, God blessed them both with a plentiful harvest.

One year the harvest was better than ever. The grains grew taller than the brothers could reach, golden and beautiful as far as the eye could see. Their wooden carts creaked under the weight of all this bounty.

As he was bringing in the last of his harvest, Judah thought to himself: "This is the best harvest I ever had. Certainly I have plenty of food for myself and my family. But Isaac lives all alone. My sons can help me raise more grain if we run short, but my poor brother has no one to help him. It is not right for me to enjoy this extra food. My brother deserves to have more."

That same evening, as Isaac brought in the last of his harvest, he thought: "This was a magnificent harvest. I have plenty of food for myself. But Judah has to provide for a wife and two sons. I live alone and have no one else to care for. It is not right for me to enjoy this extra food. My brother deserves to have more."

Late that night, each brother got out of bed and dressed quickly. Judah was careful not to wake his wife and children. He left his house and went outside to the pile of grain. He gathered a large part of the pile, placed it in his cart, and started up the side of the hill to bring this food to his brother's house.

Isaac also dressed quickly and gathered a large part of his grain to bring to his brother. He took a cart and started up the side of the hill toward his brother's house.

They both reached the top of the hill at the same time and were surprised to see the other. Realizing what had happened, they jumped out of their carts and, crying, they embraced.

God saw that act of brotherly love and said: "Blessed is the field where these brothers stand."

And many years later King Solomon built the Holy Temple on that very hill!

(Adapted from folklore)

Esau and Jacob are not the only brothers whose story is told in the Torah. Of course, there is the tale of Cain and Abel. Also, we read about Isaac and Ishmael, Joseph and his brothers, as well as Moses and Aaron. In every case, the biblical narrative reveals occasions of sibling strife. Yet, our tradition points beyond these examples of fraternal conflict toward a loftier ideal: "A brother is born to share adversity." (Proverbs 17:17) "A Tale of Two Brothers" is an apt illustration of such a relationship. Despite those clashes that occur in any sibling relationship, there is the potential bond that when forged links one's life to the other's in an intensely loving way.

Why did Judah decide to bring some of his harvest to Isaac; why did Isaac decide to bring some of his to Judah? What did the brothers realize when they saw one another at the top of the hill? Why did God bless the fields where the brothers stood? What do you know about the story of Jacob and Esau? Were they the same kind of brothers as Isaac and Judah from our story? The bible teaches us: "A brother is born to share adversity." What is adversity? What does that saying from the Bible mean? Have you ever aided your brother or sister in adversity? Have they ever aided you in adversity? What does it take to have a good relationship with brothers or sisters?

· VAYETZE ·

Then Jacob said to Laban, "Give me my wife. . . ." When morning came, there was Leah! So he said to Laban, "What is this you have done to me? I was in your service for Rachel!"   Genesis 29:21, 25

→》》 《《←

The Merchant and the Thief

MENDEL WAS A THIEF. That was his profession. Some people are doctors or lawyers. Maybe others are teachers. Mendel robbed people for a living. Since what he did made others angry, he did not stay in any one town for long. Instead, he went from place to place.

He used to say, "It is not hard to deceive people—once."

In his travels, Mendel happened upon the town of Pinsk. Once there, he found himself a place to stay and set out to see what Pinsk was like.

Well, it was Monday, market day. The dusty old town square was filled with people. There were people buying. Oh, one could buy potatoes, eggs, carrots, and beets, kerosene for the lamps, and wood for the stoves. If you wanted yarn, you went to Mottel. He had yarn. He had knitting needles as well and thread for sewing. If you wanted candles for Shabbat, you went to Feivel. He had tall candles and short candles, fat candles and thin candles. If you wanted flour for chalah and biscuits, you went to Sarah. She herself ground the grains with the help of her four children.

Mendel walked up and down the aisles of little tables and stalls. He was looking for something special—something he knew he would not find on a shelf, but something, nevertheless, he knew he would find in the marketplace.

He was looking for gossip. He wanted to know who was the richest person in town. It was not long before he found what he was looking for.

Without warning, the yelling and the screaming in the market-place stopped. There was a hush and Mendel looked around to see a big, bearded man wearing a magnificent black fur hat and long black coat. He was making his way through the crowded marketplace. As he passed by, people would whisper, "So what brings Reb Reuven, the richest man in Pinsk, to the marketplace today? Please, God, maybe he will stop and buy something from me today."

"So that is the richest man in town!" Mendel thought. "I must pay him a visit."

The next day who should stop by the home of Reb Reuven but Mendel the Thief.

"Please pardon this intrusion, Reb Reuven. I know you are an important and busy man," said Mendel. "I am a poor wandering soul who has come to Pinsk to change my fortune. It is as they say, 'When one changes his place, he changes his luck.' Tonight, I have invited Reb Mottel and his wife to dinner. I am going to ask him for a job. Although I am poor, I shall provide some meal and fill their bellies with warm food and their souls with good humor. Reb Reuven, I have come to you to take advantage of your reputation for generosity and ask if I might borrow two forks so that my guests might eat the meal I will prepare. You will have them back first thing tomorrow morning, I promise."

Reb Reuven thought to himself that this seemed like an odd request. But he was a generous man and what did two forks matter to a man with his wealth. So he gave Mendel two forks.

The next morning, Mendel reappeared at Reb Reuven's home. When Reb Reuven opened the door, he found Mendel standing there, holding a small brown bag.

"Reb Reuven, you were very kind to lend me these forks. God has rewarded you for your generosity for a miracle has happened."

With that, Mendel opened the brown bag and presented Reb Reuven not only with the two forks he had given but with two additional forks.

22

"What is this?" asked Reb Reuven. "I lent you only two forks. Why are you giving me four forks in return?"

"That is the miracle," explained Mendel. "I had placed your forks in this bag last night after my guests had left. This morning, when I lifted the bag to bring it back to you, it seemed heavier than it had the night before. When I opened it, what should I discover but four forks instead of two. Do they not say, 'The generous person will be enriched'?"

Then Mendel had the chutzpah to ask Reb Reuven for the use of two goblets. It seems Reb Mottel was not able to help him with a job and, so, he had invited Reb Feivel over for some *schnapps*. When Reb Reuven handed him two goblets, Mendel thanked him and promised to return them first thing the next day.

Early the next morning, who should be standing at Reb Reuven's door but Mendel the Thief! When Reb Reuven opened the door, he saw Mendel, holding that same brown bag.

"Reb Reuven, your generosity must be known in the highest of heavens for another miracle has occurred in your name. Behold, you gave me two goblets and I give you four in return. The Talmud teaches that 'miracles don't happen every day,' but here it has happened twice."

Reb Reuven took the four goblets from Mendel and was about to wish him *Shalom Aleichem* when Mendel made yet another request.

"God, please forgive me, but I must cast myself upon the generosity of your heart this one last time. Today, I must travel north to see Reb Shmuel of Minsk. Reb Feivel was unable to help me and now I seek the aid of Reb Shmuel. But the road to the north is long and cold. I am afraid that I might freeze before I even reach Minsk. Let your generosity extend to me this one last time so that I might borrow your fine coat and hat. Surely, they will keep me warm and Reb Shmuel will think that I am a man of fine bearing and character. I promise I will return them to you first thing tomorrow morning."

So Reb Reuven handed Mendel his coat and hat. Mendel departed and was never seen again in Pinsk. He was after Reb Reuven's coat and hat from the beginning. How could Reb Reuven be so foolish?

The righteous are righteous because they are wise as well. Reb

23

Reuven had been prepared for Mendel's final visit. When he picked up his coat and hat to bring to Mendel, he placed a bag of fleas under the brim of his hat and in the collar of his coat.

It is as they say: "God waits long—but pays with interest."

(Adapted from a chasidic parable)

According to tradition, this *sidrah* is the basis for the custom of *badeken di kalah,* "veiling of the bride." Before the wedding ceremony, the groom looks at the bride to identify her before covering her face with the veil. Because Jacob was deceived by Laban and married Leah instead of Rachel, Jewish husbands ever since have made certain they are marrying the right woman.

Deception is at the center of this biblical episode as it is in the preceding portion where Jacob deceives his father Isaac and receives the paternal blessing intended for Esau. Folklore has it that "it is not hard to deceive people—once." Eventually, however, one who practices deceit is bound to become its victim. Such was the case with Jacob and Laban. Such is the case with the thief in our story.

What does this story have to do with our Torah portion? What do you think is the moral of this story? What does it mean to deceive someone? Can you give some examples of ways one person might deceive another? Who gets hurt with deception?

· VAYISLACH ·

Looking up, Jacob saw Esau coming, accompanied by four hundred men. . . . Esau ran to greet him. He embraced him and, falling on his neck, he kissed him; and they wept.

Genesis 33:1,4

⇛ ⇚

The Greatest Gift

ISAAC AND JOSEPH were brothers. They were not friends. Pity the poor mother who had to raise them under the same roof! Isaac begrudged Joseph every success he ever had. Rather than be happy and rejoice in his brother's good fortune, Isaac became more angry and more envious. Does age transform envy into love? Perhaps in the hearts and souls of others. But as Isaac grew older his envy intensified.

Joseph had become a kind and caring man. He worked hard as a farmer and after many years his toil paid off. His fields stood full of golden grains, green vegetables, and orange, red, and yellow fruits. This harvest would make all the years of hard work worthwhile for him.

Isaac had watched his brother's fields grow rich and full of produce. He could have shared this wealth. Joseph had invited him many times to come and work the fields with him and claim part of its bounty as his own. But Joseph's generosity made Isaac even more angry.

So, Isaac devised a plan that would ruin Joseph once and for all. Very late on the night before Joseph was to harvest his fields, Isaac, with some of his mean-spirited friends, harvested Joseph's fields and sowed salt in the empty furrows so that nothing would ever again grow in that soil.

Joseph was left with nothing. He had no produce to sell. He had no land upon which to grow anything. Meanwhile, Isaac sold the grains, vegetables, and fruit for a great deal of money. He bought a big house and hired many servants.

When Joseph went to confront his brother with what he had done, Isaac had his servants throw Joseph out of his home. What was Joseph to do? He had no money and a worthless farm. He needed help. But where could he go to get it?

"Rabbi Akiva!" he cried. "Rabbi Akiva is a man of much wisdom. I will go to him and he will advise me."

So Joseph set out to see Rabbi Akiva. It was a long journey and, after many hours of walking through the hills of Judea, Joseph needed a place to rest and something to eat. Not far away he saw an orange tree and decided to stop there. As he got close to the tree, he noticed how strange a tree it was.

"I have never seen a tree like this before," he said. "One side is full of beautiful, long branches and juicy-looking oranges. But, the other side is brown and lifeless, not one orange grows there."

"Help me, please help me!" cried the tree.

"How can I help you?" Joseph asked. "I cannot even help myself. I am going to see Rabbi Akiva to ask his advice."

"Do you think you could ask Rabbi Akiva about my problem?" the orange tree asked.

"I am sure that I could. In fact, I *will* ask! I promise," pledged Joseph.

"Please take some of my oranges for your long journey," offered the tree. "Those over there on my good side are the best, sweetest oranges you will ever taste. Just don't forget me. You won't forget me, will you?"

Joseph promised not to forget his new friend and continued on his way. The oranges were as good as the tree had said they would be and they gave Joseph new energy. He walked quickly and whistled as he went.

After a few hours he came to a wide river. Joseph picked up a long branch and walked into the water to test how deep it was. Too deep! Sadly, he walked out of the water and sat down with his head in his hands as if he were going to cry.

"I'll never get to see Rabbi Akiva now," he thought.

Just then a wave of water sprayed him until he was soaking wet.

"What! Who did that?"

"I did." Joseph heard a deep, commanding voice and wiped the water from his eyes to see who was there. When he looked, he could not believe what he saw and he wiped his eyes again to make sure that he was not dreaming. There before him was the biggest, meanest-looking fish he had ever seen. It was standing on its huge tail, rising twelve feet high, right in front of Joseph.

"I did it," repeated the fish. "This is my river and no one crosses it without checking with me first. Why do you want to cross my river?"

Joseph told the fish the whole story. He explained how his brother Isaac had stolen his crops and ruined his land. He told the fish how he was going to see Rabbi Akiva to learn how to solve his problems.

"Do you think Rabbi Akiva could help me?" asked the fish. "I have had this terrible pain behind my left eye for years and years. I can't sleep and have been so grouchy that I have chased away all my friends. Please, can you ask Rabbi Akiva how I can get rid of this awful ache?"

"Of course, I will ask him," said Joseph. He could not bear to see the fish in so much pain.

"Then hop on my back and I will bring you across the river," called the fish. And he brought Joseph to the other side.

Joseph walked all the rest of that day, finally reaching B'nai B'rak as the sun was about to set. This was the home of Rabbi Akiva and his famous academy, where students from all over the land came to study with the wise and learned rabbi.

When Joseph found Akiva, the rabbi was sitting under a tree, surrounded by his students. His words were so clear, Joseph could hear every one, even though he was still far away.

"Beloved is a person in that he was created in the image of God." Joseph thought about those words. "Everyone is created in the image of God," he thought. "I guess that even my brother, Isaac, was created in the image of God."

The day's class was over and the students began to leave. Akiva noticed Joseph and motioned for him to come over.

"You appear to have a great problem that makes your soul heavy and your eyes very sad," said Akiva. "Why don't you tell me what it is that could trouble you so."

Joseph told Rabbi Akiva the whole story. He remembered his promises to the orange tree and the fish and told Akiva of their promises also.

"Well," said Akiva. "When you return to the river, look behind the left eye of the fish. And, when you return to the orange tree, search under the roots on its bad side. I think you will find what has troubled your friends. But, as for you, this visit was not necessary. It was your hard work and talent that made your first farm a success. That same ability will make anything you do successful. You are the only person who can change your fortune. I cannot do it for you. There is nothing I can give you that you do not already have. So, let me give you this teaching. It is the only gift I can give you."

Akiva looked right into Joseph's eyes. He put his right hand on Joseph's shoulder and, in a very soft voice, he said: "The most important teaching in our whole Torah is this: 'You shall love your neighbor as yourself.'"

Akiva turned from Joseph and walked away. That night, Joseph slept under the tree where Akiva taught his students.

The next day, Joseph returned to the river and checked behind the bad eye of the fish. There he found a beautiful, round pearl that had caused all the pain. The fish was so happy to be rid of his ache that he gave Joseph the pearl as a gift.

When Joseph returned to the orange tree, he searched under its roots and discovered the cause of the tree's problems. A large bag had been buried on top of the roots. No wonder the tree was not completely well! When Joseph unearthed the bag, he found it full of gold coins. The tree was so happy to have the bag off its roots that it told Joseph to keep it and all that was inside.

All that wealth enabled Joseph to buy the land he needed to start a new farm. It was not long before he had a new harvest and it was every bit as good if not even a little bit better than the harvest his brother Isaac had stolen. Isaac had spent his money quickly and was poor again. But Joseph had learned something special from Rabbi Akiva. Akiva had taught him to love others as he would love himself. So, Joseph forgave his brother and invited Isaac to come to his farm.

This time Isaac came and there he learned how to be a good

farmer. Of all the gifts that had come from his visit to Rabbi Akiva, Joseph considered the reunion with his brother to be the greatest of them all.

(Adapted from folklore)

Jacob certainly did not expect Esau to embrace him, not after having cheated Esau out of his birthright. Jacob was fearful that Esau would seek revenge. The Torah portion tells us that Jacob, afraid of Esau's anger, sent his family away to safety and prepared to meet Esau alone. According to the biblical text, Jacob wrestled with a "stranger" that night and prevailed. As a result, his name was changed to Israel. The ancients considered a change of name to be symbolic of a conversion or transformation of some kind. Perhaps, the trauma of confronting Esau compelled Jacob to do some deep soul-searching, which led to his personal midlife metamorphosis. The next day, a changed Jacob met his brother. Esau recognized this change (perhaps Esau had changed, too) and a reconciliation took place. The brothers embraced.

Why would Isaac ruin his brother's crops? What did Akiva teach Joseph? What did this lesson have to do with Joseph and his brother Isaac? What did Joseph consider to be the greatest of all his gifts? Why was this so? Compare this story and our Torah portion? Why do you think that Esau embraced Jacob when he might have attacked him instead?

· VAYESHEV ·

Now Israel loved Joseph best of all his sons . . . and he had made him an ornamented tunic. And when his brothers saw that their father loved him more than any of his brothers, they hated him so that they could not speak a friendly word to him.   Genesis 37:3,4

→》》 《《←

Itzi and Pitzi

A<small>M I HUNGRY!</small>" Itzi the dog had not eaten in two days. He had come to the marketplace in search of food.

"What's that over there? Did that lady just drop some food? Oh, I hope so. It must be."

Itzi rushed over to where he had seen the lady drop the food. He did not want anyone else to get there first.

"Cheese. A piece of cheese. How wonderful! I love cheese. This piece is fresh and it's all mine." And Itzi took the piece of cheese in his mouth and started off to find a place to eat his dinner.

"Am I hungry!" Pitzi the cat was wandering up and down the aisles of the marketplace, looking for scraps of food. He had not eaten in two days.

He turned a corner and was about to head down another aisle when something fell from the table above him, just missing his head.

"What's that! Hey, be careful up there!" he shouted. "A guy could get hurt around here," he thought. And then he saw what had fallen.

"Cheese. It's a piece of cheese. How wonderful! I love cheese."

It was a pretty big piece of cheese and Pitzi had trouble picking it up at first. But he was so hungry that nothing could stop him from carrying it to a place where he could eat it all alone, savoring every last delicious bite by himself.

Maybe the people in the marketplace did not notice Pitzi as he tried to carry his piece of cheese. The market is a busy place. People don't notice even if they run over another person or step on someone else's foot. How are they going to notice a little cat carrying a piece of cheese which no one would want anyway?

Maybe the people in the marketplace did not notice Pitzi, but Itzi did. He saw that cat and that piece of cheese.

"That piece of cheese is twice the size of mine. I am twice the size of that puny little cat. That piece of cheese should be mine." Itzi wanted Pitzi's piece of cheese and he wanted it so badly that he left his own piece of cheese behind on the ground and rushed right over to where Pitzi sat preparing to eat his dinner.

"That cheese is not yours. I saw it first," declared Itzi. He knew he was lying but that did not matter.

"It is not your cheese," shouted Pitzi. "I was all alone when this piece of cheese fell right out of the sky and almost killed me. It is my cheese. Now go away and leave me alone."

"I will not go away. Not until you give me that cheese," barked Itzi.

"I will not give you my cheese. I will not," screeched Pitzi.

In the middle of all this confusion, who should come strolling along but Ketzi the fox. He was a clever one, that Ketzi. He knew it and the other animals knew it, too. When he saw Itzi and Pitzi and that hunk of cheese, he thought of a plan right away.

"Wow, what is going on here!" Ketzi shouted as he came near to where Itzi and Pitzi stood arguing.

"This thief wants to steal my cheese," cried Pitzi the cat.

"No, that thief wants to steal my cheese," yelled Itzi the dog.

"Maybe, I can be of help," offered Ketzi. "Tell me what happened."

So, Itzi and Pitzi each told Ketzi their stories. Ketzi listened to each one and then gave his opinion.

"Let me propose a solution," said Ketzi. "I am going to divide this big piece of cheese. Pitzi, you know that it is too big for you to eat by yourself. So, let me give you this piece and I will give Itzi what is left."

Ketzi divided the piece of cheese so that Pitzi the cat had the biggest slice and Itzi had a tiny slice.

"Wait a minute," cried Itzi. "That cat still has a piece that is too big. You have given me such a small piece of cheese that I will die from hunger and that will be on your head."

"You are right," said Ketzi the fox. "I did give Pitzi too large a piece." So Ketzi bit off a piece of Pitzi's cheese.

"Now you have really done it," screeched Pitzi. "You have taken a piece of my cheese and now that dog has more than I have. It was my cheese to begin with. I saw it first. I should have the bigger piece."

"You are right," said Ketzi. He turned to Itzi's piece of cheese and bit off a piece. "Now Pitzi, your piece is bigger than Itzi's once more."

"Oh, no you don't," shouted Itzi. "This is not fair. I am twice the size of that puny cat and I should have twice the cheese."

"You have a point," said Ketzi. So he turned and bit off another piece of Pitzi's cheese so that Itzi's piece was now larger.

Back and forth this argument went. First Pitzi would claim his piece ought to be larger and then Itzi would claim that his piece ought to be larger. Each time Itzi or Pitzi would complain, Ketzi would bite off another piece of cheese.

Finally, Ketzi had eaten enough. He was full. Itzi and Pitzi were left with tiny bits of cheese, not enough to make a snack, let alone a whole meal. Ketzi walked away with a smile on his face, leaving Itzi and Pitzi behind, as hungry as they were at the beginning.

A folk saying tells us: "Envy is like a disease—it consumes the soul." It certainly consumed the souls of Joseph's brothers, igniting the fires of hatred within them and leading them to cast their brother into a pit. Subsequently, a caravan of Ishmaelites discovered Joseph abandoned in the pit. They rescued him from his subterranean prison and sold him to a group of Midianite traders who, in turn, sold him into the service of an Egyptian named Potiphar, a courtier of the pharaoh. Thus begins the history of our ancestors in Egypt. In our story, envy and greed deprive Itzi and Pitzi of a meal.

What is the problem between Itzi and Pitzi? What is Ketzi's solution to their problem? If you were walking by and saw Itzi and Pitzi arguing, what advice would you have given them? There is a Jewish saying: "The fish on another person's plate is very appetizing." What do you think that means? What does that saying have to do with our story? What do you think Joseph's brothers could have learned from our story?

After two years' time, Pharaoh dreamed that he was standing by the Nile, when out of the Nile there came up seven cows, handsome and sturdy, and they grazed in the reed grass. But presently, seven other cows came up from the Nile close behind them, ugly and gaunt, and stood beside the cows on the bank of the Nile; and the ugly gaunt cows ate up the seven handsome sturdy cows. And Pharaoh awoke. He fell asleep and dreamed a second time . . . Then Pharaoh awoke: it was a dream! Genesis 41:1–5,7

⟶⟶⟶ ⟵⟵⟵

The Nebech's Dream

WHAT WAS THE LAST DREAM you remembered? When was the last time you had a dream that was so real that it haunted you all day long after you awakened?

Naphtali had such a dream. Only he was visited by that dream not once, but for seven nights in a row! Even on the Sabbath, he could not escape it. Each time it was exactly the same: He stood on the main street in Cracow watching the comings-and-goings of the horse-drawn carriages with their wealthy patrons sitting inside chatting merrily away. Oh, how he longed to be among the nobility and to ride in a carriage like those! Suddenly, one of the carriages would come to a halt. Its driver would dismount from his seat and walk to the side of the shiny black carriage. He opened the door and out stepped a tall man, garbed in black from head to toe. The man's face was covered with a black mask and his hands were covered with black leather gloves. Without a word the faceless figure would approach Naphtali and hand him a note. It read: "Go to the king's palace and dig beneath the bridge which leads to its gates. There you will find a treasure of riches beyond your fondest hopes." Then the figure in black would return to his carriage and ride away.

Naphtali awakened each night at this point in his dream. Sweating and breathing very quickly, he would lie in bed and think about the man in black. It seemed so real that he expected to find the man seated in the chair across the room. But it was only a dream. A dream that came to Naphtali every night for seven nights in a row!

If Naphtali had been a wealthy man, he probably could have forgotten that dream. Ah, but Naphtali was a *nebech*. There's a saying about a *nebech*: "When a *nebech* leaves a room, you feel as if someone came in." Naphtali was that kind of a poor, unfortunate soul who would always get to the market after the last potato was sold. He would come to *shul* after the last seat had been taken. He would be the one to find the only piece of herring with the bones. A woodcutter by trade, Naphtali managed to make enough of a living to keep his wife and children alive. But, he wanted more for his family. Somewhere out there in the streets of Cracow was the answer, and Naphtali was determined to find it.

But that dream still haunted him. What about his dream?

Naphtali decided that maybe this was his chance to strike it rich. So, he decided to go off to the king's palace and dig for his treasure.

When he reached the bridge leading to the king's palace, he noticed that there were two guards on patrol. How was he going to dig for his treasure if these guards were watching? Wouldn't they want to know what he was doing? Wouldn't they try to stop him? Wouldn't they try to keep the treasure for themselves?

Naphtali sat down at the foot of the bridge and thought about what to do. He sat there for hours, waiting to see if the guards would take a break. No luck. When these guards were through patrolling, two other guards came to take their places. There was no way for him to dig unnoticed.

After a while, one of the guards saw Naphtali sitting on the hill by the bridge.

"You there," he called to Naphtali. "What are you doing here? State your business."

Naphtali did not know what to say. Should he tell the guard what he was really doing there? What else could he say?

So, Naphtali told the guard all about his dream.

The guard laughed. "If I believed every dream I had, I would have gone to the home of a woodcutter to dig under the floor of his house. One night I dreamed that a huge treasure lay hidden under the stove in the home of some Jewish woodcutter named Naphtali. Now, who ever heard of anything so ridiculous?"

As soon as he heard the guard's story, Naphtali turned on his heels and ran home as fast as his legs would carry him. He burst through his front door and pushed aside the iron stove, without noticing that it was red hot and full of burning wood. Furiously, he began shoveling in the spot where the stove usually stood. Naphtali's wife knew she had married a *nebech,* but now she thought he had become a full-fledged *meshugener.* Sarah watched in wide-eyed amazement as her husband destroyed her kitchen floor.

Clank! Naphtali's shovel hit upon something metallic. With unrestrained glee, Naphtali bent down and hoisted up a rusted metal box, filled with gold and silver and diamonds and rubies.

From that day on, Naphtali never had his dream again. Naphtali was no longer a *nebech.* The answer to his prayers had been right under his own nose all these years. Maybe, I should say that the answer had been under his own stove all these years.

(Adapted from folklore)

In the ancient world, dreams were regarded as secret codes that held important messages from divine sources. Special individuals, professional dream interpreters, possessed the key to unlock them. Apparently, Joseph was one of them; Daniel was another. Today, we do not consider dreams to be divine communications but indications of unconscious desires or anxieties. Thus we employ psychotherapists to decode the secrets of our dreams. Nevertheless, we remain as fascinated by dreams as were Joseph and the ancient world.

It has been said: "In bed thoughts come to your mind so that you may know the thoughts of your heart." What do you think that means? Do you think that dreams can teach us anything important? Can you recall the last dream you had? Make believe that you are Joseph and interpret your dream. What is the lesson to be learned from our story? Why do you think Naphtali found the treasure buried in his home only *after* he returned from his journey?

· VAYIGASH ·

Then Joseph said to his brothers, "Come forward to me."
And when they came forward, he said, "I am your brother
Joseph, he whom you sold into Egypt. Now, do not be
distressed or reproach yourselves because you sold me
hither. . . . He kissed all his brothers and wept upon them;
only then were his brothers able to talk to him.

Genesis 45:4–5,15

Forgiveness Comes with Kindness

SHMUEL BEN YITZHAK was a chasid of the Medzibozer Rebbe.
He attended all of the rebbe's Torah classes called *shiurim,* in
which the rebbe spoke of Abraham and Isaac, Sarah and Rebecca,
and all the great sages of our history. In Shmuel's eyes, the rebbe
could do nothing wrong, and everything he said was as true as
if the Holy One personally had uttered them.

During one particular *shiur,* Shmuel heard the rebbe say that
the Ladier Rebbe disagreed with him about some matter of *hala-
chah.* Shmuel could not believe that anyone, even the Ladier Rebbe,
would dare disagree with his beloved rebbe. So, Shmuel traveled
to Ladier to find the rebbe and put him in his place.

"No one can question the opinion of my rebbe and get away
with it!" Shmuel exclaimed. And, the more he thought about
the arrogance of the Ladier Rebbe, the more angry he became.

When Shmuel arrived in Ladier, he went straight to the *shtibl* in which the Ladier Rebbe taught. He burst into the room and found a dozen students seated on benches around a long wooden table, at whose head sat the Ladier Rebbe himself. Surprised and taken aback by this abrupt interruption, there was a strange silence in the room while all eyes focused upon Shmuel, the intruder.

There, in front of all the students, Shmuel insulted the Ladier Rebbe and told him how arrogant he was to dare to disagree with the sainted and venerable Rebbe of Medzibozer.

When the Medzibozer Rebbe heard what had happened, he sent for Shmuel immediately. Expecting praise for his loyalty, Shmuel was severely shocked to hear his rebbe's rebuke.

"You must return to Ladier and ask the rebbe's forgiveness," instructed the Medzibozer Rebbe.

Shmuel did as his teacher said. He returned to Ladier and sought out the rebbe. He begged his forgiveness in a very humble and contrite manner. The Ladier Rebbe looked at Shmuel with very kind and sparkling eyes and said, "You may only win my forgiveness with an act of kindness. Your words do not suffice."

Not long after his visit with the Ladier Rebbe, Shmuel's daughter became very sick. No one seemed able to help her recover. Things looked very bleak indeed. Upset and frustrated, Shmuel left his home and began walking through the forest that surrounded the town of Medzibozer.

After several hours of wandering around, Shmuel came upon a small hut in the midst of a clearing. Though he had spent many hours in this forest before, he had never come upon this clearing nor had he ever seen this wooden hut.

As he came closer to the hut, he heard the sound of crying. Quickening his pace, Shmuel hurried to the door. There, on a bed of straw, lay a woman about to give birth. She was all alone, no one else was to be found in the house or anywhere outside. Shmuel rushed inside and wiped the sweat from her brow. He spoke softly and soothingly to her, telling her that everything was going to be alright. She was not alone. He was here to help her.

Shmuel was true to his word. Not until the baby was born did he leave the woman's side. Then, once the baby was washed and cradled in her mother's arms, Shmuel went for some wood for the stove so that he could boil some more water for soup.

With arms full of branches, Shmuel returned to the hut. It

was gone! Thinking that he had gotten lost, Shmuel doubled back upon his path and searched for the small wooden hut. Hours and hours of searching, but the hut was nowhere to be found.

Confused and exhausted, Shmuel headed home to see how his daughter was feeling. When he arrived back home, he found his daughter up and about. There was no longer any sign of fever. There was a healthy tinge of red in her cheeks, and she was full of life.

Shmuel had been forgiven. Such is the power of forgiveness achieved through kindness.

(Adapted from chasidic folklore)

Joseph had the opportunity, the means, and the motive to punish his brothers for selling him into slavery. Yet, as the folk saying goes: "If you take revenge, you will regret it; if you forgive, you will rejoice." Joseph forgave. Putting aside old grudges is a difficult thing to do. In fact, sometimes we act as if we were putting our grudges aside when we forgive others, but our pretense is hollow and our forgiveness is insincere. Others see through us right away. So, mere lip service is not enough. It is ultimately the way we behave towards others that shows if we truly forgive them or not.

In our story, Shmuel discovers that very same lesson. The Ladier Rebbe might simply have forgiven him, but Shmuel's apology seemed feigned. It was only through a special deed that Shmuel found forgiveness.

What does this story have to do with our Torah portion? Joseph forgave his brothers right away, but why didn't the Ladier Rebbe forgive Shmuel at first? Do you agree with the rebbe's response to Shmuel? What would you have done if you were the rebbe? Is it always enough just to say that you are sorry? How can someone else tell that you are serious about your apology? What did Shmuel do finally to receive the rebbe's forgiveness? What do you do when you really want to apologize to your parents, your brothers or sisters, or your friends? How do you make them see that you are really sincere about your apology?

· VAYECHI ·

When Jacob finished his instructions to his sons, he drew his feet into the bed and, breathing his last, he was gathered to his people.   Genesis 49:33

≫≫ ≪≪

Honi and the Carob Tree

Many years ago, in the land of Judah, there lived a man named Honi Hama'agel. *Ha-ma'agel* is a nickname; it means "the circle-drawer." In Judah, where Honi lived, there is a dry season and a rainy season. If the rainy season does not come on time, the crops do not receive enough rainfall to grow properly. It is awful to see drooping corn or sagging wheat or wrinkled tomatos. So, rain in its proper season is very important. One year, the rains were very late in coming. Honi saw what was happening to the crops all around him and decided he was going to do something about it. But what could be done?

Honi stepped out into the middle of an empty field and picked up a stick. Using the pointed end, he drew a circle in the dirt. Then he dropped the stick and lifted his head to the heavens.

"Ruler of the universe," cried Honi, speaking directly to God, "I am Honi. You know me. I am not a great man, but I am a pious man and I have studied Your laws and I have lived the kind of life You have commanded me to live as a Jew. I have stood among my friends in the synagogue and have joined them in prayer for the rain, just as one is supposed to do at this time in this season."

Honi took a breath. It was not every day that he spoke to God this way.

"I have drawn a circle in the earth which has become parched

41

because the rains have not come. I will not leave this circle until our prayers for rain have been answered. Ruler of the universe, I know You are just and compassionate. Will You not bless those who strive to walk in Your ways with the rains that will bring life to this soil and food to those who are hungry!"

And Honi stopped speaking. He stood, motionless and silent, his eyes never blinking as he gazed into the depths of the heavens.

Then, thunder crashed throughout the skies and clouds welled up from out of nowhere. Down came the rain, torrents and torrents of rain. Honi looked up and smiled through the raindrops which washed his face. He reached down and picked up his stick and left the field.

From that day on, Honi was called *ha-ma'agel,* "the circle-drawer."

The rains had come and gone. Jerusalem and the surrounding hills were lush with the flowers and blossoms of spring. Honi saddled his donkey and went out into the Judean hills.

The sun was warm—just warm enough to feel good after the chill of winter. As his donkey picked its way up the trails in the foothills, Honi could smell the aroma of spring and could see the green grass, the blossoming cactus flowers, and the fruit trees bringing forth the green balls that would become apples and oranges.

Along the way, Honi came upon a man digging in the earth by the side of the trail. There did not seem to be a farm here. There was neither an orchard nor an orange grove. Yet, this man worked, digging his spade deep into the earth.

"*Shalom Aleichem,*" called Honi to the man.

"*Aleichem Shalom,*" responded the man.

"I am Honi, come on a ride with my donkey to gaze upon the birth of God's world."

"And I am Abba ben Shlomo," said the man.

"Why does Abba ben Shlomo stand here in the middle of the Judean hills digging a hole?"

"I am digging a hole so that I might plant a carob tree."

"Excuse me for asking," Honi began, "but you are not a boy anymore and everyone knows that it takes many, many years for a carob tree to grow. Do you expect to confound your fate and live to see this tree all grown?"

"Perhaps, I will live so long," replied Abba ben Shlomo. "But

42

maybe I will not be so fortunate. Still, I will plant the tree. When I was born, I entered the world with beautiful trees and wonderful fruits and luscious vegetables and lush, green fields. Is it not my responsibility to make sure that my children and their children shall enjoy all those same wonderful things? I am poor and cannot give them many sheep or a great home. But, I can leave them something. So, I stand here in the spring sun and plant this tree."

Honi bade Abba ben Shlomo good-bye and mounted the back of his donkey. He had learned a very important lesson of life and death.

(Adapted from the Talmud)

Rashi, the great medieval commentator, once said: "Naked a person comes into this world and naked he leaves it . . . he carries away nothing, except the deeds he leaves behind." After a full life, Jacob had an opportunity to bequeath to his children the fruits of his labors. Did he distribute jewelry, cattle, land, or coins among his heirs? That was not his legacy to them. Instead, as Jacob lie upon his death bed, he asked each of his sons to come before him to receive a blessing. These blessings were combinations of prayers, warnings, parables, personality assessments, and instructions, representing the wisdom of a lifetime. These were his last gifts to his children. Similarly, in our story, Honi meets a man who is in the midst of preparing his children's inheritance. As a result of this encounter, Honi learns a lesson about life and death.

What is an inheritance? What kinds of things does one usually inherit? What is a legacy? How does Jacob's legacy to his children differ from the kind of legacy usually found in an inheritance? Why do you think he chose to give each of his children a blessing instead of something else? What kind of legacy is the old man in our story leaving for his children? What do you think Honi learned from the old man?

The daughter of Pharaoh came down to bathe in the Nile.
. . . She spied the basket among the reeds and sent her
slave girl to fetch it. . . . When the child grew up, she
brought him to Pharaoh's daughter, who made him her
son. She named him Moses, explaining, "I drew him out
of the water." Exodus 2:5,10

➤➤➤ ⫷⫷⫷

Moses and Pharaoh's Crown

NOT MANY YOUNG BOYS get to grow up in the house of the
pharaoh of Egypt. Moses did. Ever since Pharaoh's daughter,
Bithiah, had found Moses floating along the Nile in that fragile
little basket, she had cared for him as if he were her own child.
He lived in the palace, played with the children of the other princes
and princesses, and ate all his meals with the royal family.

One night at dinner, Moses climbed down off his mother's
lap and crawled on top of the table. He made a mess of the
pudding and the fruits but everyone laughed. Moses smiled back
at the sound of all that laughter, but he really did not know
what all the ruckus was about. Everything on that table was
like a toy to him. He picked up the apples and tossed them on
the floor. He dipped his hand in the pudding and smeared it
across his face so that it looked as if this two-year-old baby suddenly grew a moustache—and a cockeyed one at that.

Then Moses crawled in front of Pharaoh who was delighted
with the explorations of his adopted grandson. Suddenly, Moses
reached up and grabbed the crown off Pharaoh's head. He looked
at all the shiny stones and the gleaming metal. When he tried to

place it on his own head, it fell right over his tiny head and rested on his shoulders. He thought this was funny, too. But no one else was laughing now. No one was allowed to touch Pharaoh's crown.

Bala'am, one of Pharaoh's ministers, called out, "O mighty Pharaoh, beware that child, for he seeks not only to take the crown from your head but the throne from where you sit as well."

"That's not true," cried Bithiah.

"Bala'am, Bala'am, be reasonable," said the pharaoh. "Am I not the same man who defeated the Hittites and the Hurrians? Moses is only a child. How can this wonderful child pose a threat to me?"

"Do you not remember the dream you had several days ago? You awoke full of fear and bathed in sweat. A demon had come to Egypt to wrest your throne from you. Yet, when we asked you to describe this demon to us, you said that you could not recall his features for he was clothed in darkness. Mighty Pharaoh, this child is the demon in disguise. He has come to Pharaoh's palace and taken the form of an innocent child in a diabolical attempt to deceive you!"

Bithiah protested to her father that Bala'am's words were nonsense, but Pharaoh remembered his nightmare, recalling the fear that it had planted in his heart. If the demon had taken the guise of this child, then the child must die.

Bithiah wept bitterly. "This is my son. No demon has possessed his soul. Bala'am lies. Where is his proof?"

Pharaoh looked upon his daughter. Her words and her tears touched him. Then he looked to his grandson who sat in the middle of the table, still playing with the crown, completely unaware that his fate hung on the next words his grandfather would utter.

"Bala'am, devise a test. Give me proof that the demon resides in the body of Moses and I will do all that you ask," said Pharaoh.

So it was that Bala'am designed his test. Early the next morning, Moses was brought before Pharaoh and placed at one end of a long table. At the other end of the table, there rested two silver pots. One was filled with sparkling jewels. The other was filled with hot stones whose red hot warmth made them glow like rubies.

"Pharaoh, here is your test," announced Bala'am. "If the child crawls to the pot with the stones and takes from its contents, then he is free of the demon. If he should crawl to the other pot and remove one of your jewels, then he is after your wealth and your crown and must be killed as you have ordered."

"So it must be," declared Pharaoh. His heart was heavy as he watched young Moses crawl along the length of the table. Bithiah held her breath and squeezed her fingers into a fist.

Moses moved across the table. Weren't these two pots filled with pretty things! Which to play with first? When he arrived at the other end of the table, he stopped. For a long moment, he hesitated and then he reached for—the pot with the jewels. As Moses was about to take one of the precious stones, Gabriel, one of God's most trusted angels, swept down from the heavens and caught Moses by his wrist. Quickly, he brought it over to the pot filled with the gleaming hot stones. "Two angels accompany everyone." Gabriel and Raphael had accompanied Moses from the day he was born. It was Raphael who had guided Moses' basket down the Nile to where Bithiah had found him. It was Gabriel now who placed Moses' tiny hand in the pot of hot stones.

Moses picked up one of the stones and placed it to his mouth before he could feel how hot it was. Immediately, his lips were singed and he dropped the stone.

He shrieked in pain and began to cry hysterically.

"Quick, bring him to the royal physician," cried Pharaoh. "And bring in the guards. Bala'am, you have brought harm to my grandson and you must pay for his pain."

From that day ever after, Moses spoke with great difficulty. His lips never healed completely. Years later, Aaron, his true brother, would speak for him when Moses returned to Egypt to bring his people out of bondage.

But that is another story.

(Adapted from the Midrash)

Our story, a parable, is based on a tale from the Midrash. It reflects the rabbinic imagination, which wondered what it was like for Moses to grow up in the palace of Pharaoh. Despite his future greatness, the Moses depicted in the story is a normal, playful infant. In fact, his playfulness gets him into trouble. Despite his pedestrian beginning, Moses becomes one of the great heroes of our people.

Who are other Jewish heroes? Who are heroes today? What does it take to be a hero? What does Moses do in later life to become a hero? What kinds of mitzvot can one perform to become a hero in the lives of others? Are there Jews in the world today who need a hero to save them?

The Lord spoke to Moses, saying, "Go and tell Pharaoh king of Egypt to let the Israelites depart from his land."

Exodus 6:10–11

⇻⇻⇻ ⇺⇺⇺

Moses and Aaron before Pharaoh

MOSES AND AARON arrived in Egypt and went directly to Pharaoh's court. It was the hugest palace in the world: almost as tall as a mountain, almost as wide as the Nile, and filled with more gold and silver than King Solomon's mines.

Ambassadors from every kingdom on earth were there, asking favors from the mighty pharaoh of Egypt, the mightiest empire on earth. Each brought a special gift from his country to give to Pharaoh as a present. The ambassador from India brought bags and bags of spices. The ambassador from Ethiopia brought a basket filled with diamonds. The ambassador from Greece brought bottles of pure olive oil. The ambassador from Babylonia brought carpets and cloth spun from the finest gold.

When Pharaoh's guard asked Moses and Aaron what they had brought to Pharaoh, Moses replied: "We have nothing to give Pharaoh except a warning from God."

"You have no gifts for Pharaoh and, yet, you expect to get in to see him?" And the guard began to laugh at the thought of these two desert bedouins who had come empty-handed to speak with Pharaoh.

"Not only have you no presents for Pharaoh, you also have the nerve to come here to give the mighty Pharaoh a warning," said the guard. He laughed so hard that his laughter echoed all through the hallways of the palace. Soon other guards heard the commotion and came over to see what was the matter.

When they heard what Moses and Aaron had said, they all began to laugh riotously and slap one another in the back. "Can you imagine what Pharaoh would say if he heard their request!" cried one of the guards. "What if we told him and shared our joke," suggested another. "Maybe he would find it as funny as we do. It might cheer him up."

So, it was decided. Leaving Moses and Aaron behind, the guards entered Pharaoh's court and shared their joke with him. Pharaoh, too, laughed so hard that he almost fell off his throne. He was so curious about the kind of men who had come to him with such a preposterous request that he instructed his guards to bring Moses and Aaron before him.

Pharaoh recognized Moses right away.

"Moses, Moses, we meet again. The last time we saw each other, you were being exiled from Egypt in disgrace. Now you come to see me, acting like a court jester, with quite a joke to tell. Let me see if I have this right," said Pharaoh. "You have seen all the other ambassadors who have been here with their gifts, and yet you come to see me with nothing except some kind of warning from a God no one has ever seen." And Pharaoh let out a loud laugh.

"My brother Aaron and I have come to tell you that the God of Abraham, Isaac, and Jacob commands that you 'Let our people go!'"

"What was that name?" asked Pharaoh as he grabbed the Royal List of Foreign Gods from his advisor. "The God of Abraham and who. . .?"

"The God of Abraham, Isaac, and Jacob has instructed us to come here and lead our people from slavery to freedom," announced Moses.

"We have no such god on our list," said Pharaoh. "Your God who cannot be seen does not appear on our list. I, Pharaoh, who am a god and whose father is the sun says now that you two had better go before my patience wears thin."

But Moses did not move.

"If you are a god and your father is the sun, then watch the might of the true God of the universe." Moses walked over to the window and threw back the drapes. Pharaoh and all his court-iers watched as a huge cloud drifted through the sky and covered the sun.

"If a cloud, which is not a god, can block the sun, what does it say of the might of Pharaoh?"

And Moses raised his staff to the heavens and cried, "There is but one God who created the heavens and the earth, who created day and night, who created the wind and the rain, the sun and the clouds."

Suddenly, clouds formed throughout the sky—so many clouds that the light of the sun could not be seen and the earth was filled with darkness, like night.

"Now, Pharaoh," called Moses, "who is the jester and who is the true ruler?" Moses and Aaron left the court amidst the shouts of Pharaoh.

"Guards, get them! Get them!" But the sudden darkness had terrified the guards. They were too frightened to move. Moses and Aaron left unharmed, but they knew they would have to see Pharaoh again. God's people were not yet free.

(Adapted from the Midrash)

In our Torah portion, a great confrontation takes place. Moses and Aaron come before Pharaoh to ask him to let their people go. Pharaoh, of course, knows nothing of God. I. L. Peretz once said: "One who has no God seeks idols for himself." Worse yet, Pharaoh's conceit is so exaggerated that he believes himself to be a god. Such hubris makes some human beings think that they stand above the rules and standards by which all the rest of human-ity must live. Tyranny often results: This might be tyranny in government, or tyranny in the workplace, or tyranny in the family. Tyranny knows no bounds and is not restricted to pharaohs and other despots. Greek tragedy has taught us that hubris often precip-itates a downfall. Pharaoh glimpses his own fall in the encounter described in this *sidrah*.

Why did the guards laugh when Moses and Aaron told them they wanted to see Pharaoh? Do you think Moses and Aaron were afraid of Pharaoh? Explain your answer. What was the point of the lesson Moses taught Pharaoh by making the clouds cover the sun? Can people like Pharaoh be gods? What makes our God different from the idols of the Egyptians? What does the last sentence of the story mean? When would Moses and Pharaoh meet again?

· BO ·

You shall observe this [Passover] as an institution for all time. . . . And when your children ask you, "What do you mean by this rite?" you shall say, "It is the passover sacrifice to the Lord. . . ."   Exodus 12:24,26–27

⟫⟫ ⟪⟪

The Bird of Paradise

YOU HAVE NEVER SEEN a bird like this in all your life! Have you ever seen an eagle spread its wings across the sky? This magnificient bird had a greater wingspan. Have you ever seen the brilliant colors of the peacock? This glorious creature displayed more colors, with more vivid intensity than the peacock. Have you ever seen a rooster strut his stuff in front of his clucking admirers? This regal bird made the wind stop and take notice when he paraded by.

One fine day, this bird of paradise swooped in upon the town of Meshugg. It was as if the sun had been eclipsed, for darkness suddenly blanketed the face of the earth at midday. So expansive was the breadth of his wings that the sun was completely hidden.

You can bet that the Meshuggites stopped what they were doing to turn their attention to the sky. Awestruck, they marveled at the great bird as it circled the town once, then again, and then again. The Meshuggites stood absolutely still and simply followed the bird with their eyes. Mendel the Meshuggite watched as did his wife, Miriam the Meshuggite, as did their son and daughter, Moshe and Mindel the Meshuggites. The heads of all the Meshuggites swiveled round and round on their necks like *dreidlach*.

Finally, the bird came to rest on the very top of the very tallest tree in Meshugg. It was an old tree with huge branches, but even the powerful, thick branches bent under the weight of the great bird.

All the Meshuggites hurried over to the tree. There was Mendel and Menachem, Miriam and Malka, Mottel and Mordecai, Minna and Mattl, Meir and Meshullam, Melech and Mannie.

"Did you ever see a bird like that before?" asked Mannie to anyone and to no one at the same time.

"I'd have soup for a year," mumbled Minna.

"The town which had a bird like that would be famous," said Mottel.

"Mottel, you're right," cried Mendel. "When I travel to Warsaw or Minsk or Pinsk and tell people that I am Mendel of Meshugg, they look at me and say, 'Mendel of what?' No one has ever heard of our town. No one ever comes to visit. Minna, does anyone but your friends here in Meshugg come to your stall in the market to buy your square eggs?"

Minna shook her head no.

"And you, Mannie, when was the last time you had a visitor in your roofless inn?"

"Where else can you find an inn which lets you sleep under the stars, even in winter?" replied Mannie. "All those other fancy, shmancy places give you four walls, a bed, a fireplace, and a ceiling. Who wants that? If a person wanted that, wouldn't he just stay at home?"

All the Meshuggites nodded in approval of Mannie's logic. When they want a vacation they don't leave town. They go to Mannie's roofless inn.

Soon, everyone began to realize that business would pick up and Meshugg would become famous if only they could capture this incredible bird.

Mendel had an idea. They would make a human ladder and get the bird down from the tree. So, he lined everyone up in size places. The smallest would go on the bottom and the tallest of the tall would go on top. This way, Mordecai, the tallest man in Meshugg, would be at the top of the human ladder so he could reach the bird. After all, what good would it do if the smallest Meshuggite were on the top? How could tiny Moshe reach the bird when Mordecai was a full ten hands taller?

So, little Moshe leaned against the tree on the very bottom.

Then Mindel came and stood upon his shoulders. Then Malka climbed on, followed by Miriam, and Mattl, and Minna—and down came the human ladder. Moshe simply collapsed under the weight of the others.

Obviously, Mendel was not so smart. Mannie had another idea. Since Moshe could not hold the others, why not place a large trunk on the bottom and let the others climb on top of it.

So the Meshuggites placed a huge, black trunk on the bottom of the human ladder. This time, the Meshuggites made it to Mottel before the ladder collapsed. Obviously, Mindel was too weak. She would have to be replaced. Out came another trunk.

And so it went. One by one, each Meshuggite was replaced with a trunk until the pile of trunks had risen almost high enough to reach the bird. All that remained now was for Mordecai to climb the pile of trunks, reach the bird, and capture it for the Meshuggites.

He started his ascent; one by one he climbed upon those trunks. Higher and higher he went. Within moments he would reach the bird.

At the bottom of this pile was Meir's trunk. It bore all the weight of the other trunks plus the weight of Mordecai, who stood way up at the top. As Mordecai strained to reach closer to the bird, the lid of Meir's trunk began to break. This was Meir's one and only trunk. It was the centerpiece of his home. He became more and more upset at the sight of its impending ruin until, finally, he ran to the pile and snatched his trunk out from under the others.

"I do not care about your bird or your plan. You're not going to ruin my trunk," he cried. And, with that, all the trunks came tumbling down, one after the other, after the other, and Mordecai, too.

Never was such a loud crash heard in Meshugg. It truly must have been thunderous for its force knocked the great bird from its perch, causing it to fly away to find a safer and much more quiet place to take a breather.

The great bird was not seen ever again in Meshugg or in any of the other neighboring towns. To this day, Meshugg remains unknown and the Meshuggites unknown.

(Adapted from a chasidic tale)

There are many lessons to be learned from the celebration of Passover. Certainly, one could talk about civil rights, religious freedom, or the mistreatment of other human beings. The story of the "Four Children" found in the *Haggadah* suggests one other theme: separating oneself from one's people. The wicked child is called wicked precisely becuse this child asks about the seder as an outsider might: "What do *you* mean by this right?" By using "you" instead of "we," this child stands separate and apart from the celebration. Our tradition teaches that one is not to separate from the community. In "The Bird of Paradise," Meir the Meshuggite brings down the whole human ladder when he pulls out; so, too, the Jewish community falls apart when Jews decide they want no part of Jewish life.

Children know about belonging to groups. To what groups, clubs, organizations, or teams do they belong? What happens to those bodies when people become inactive and do not care? What kinds of ways do Jews show that they are part of the Jewish people? How do they and their families show that they are involved in Jewish life?

· BESHALACH ·

The waters turned back and covered the chariots and the horsemen—Pharaoh's entire army that had followed after them into the sea; not one of them remained.

Exodus 14:28

→)) ((←

Setting Free the Captive

Rabbi Zusya had traveled many miles that day. He had walked from one side of Galicia to the other in order to raise money to ransom the Jews that had been taken captive in raids called pogroms. It is a mitzvah to set captives free, and Rabbi Zusya would not rest until he had fulfilled it to the best of his ability.

As the sun set, Rabbi Zusya looked for some place to stay for the night. He was exhausted and hungry. He trudged ahead as darkness slowly covered the countryside. Finally, he came upon an inn.

He walked through the doorway and entered a large room where a few travelers were sitting and eating. Because Rabbi Zusya wanted to use the money he raised to free Jewish prisoners, he ate very little and took whichever room was the least expensive.

Hanging from the ceiling of the large room was a bird cage, filled with all kinds of birds. Rabbi Zusya recognized humming birds, bluebirds, sparrows, woodpeckers, owls, and even an eagle. They looked so lifeless locked up in that cage. There was no room for them to fly and stretch their wings. They could not even look out through the window to see the countryside. Rabbi Zusya could not help but feel their pain.

When the innkeeper left the room, Rabbi Zusya climbed on one of the tables and opened the cage. The birds saw their chance and flew out to freedom. They swooped down through the room and out the door.

The sound of the birds brought the innkeeper back to the room. When he saw what had happened, he demanded to know who was responsible for freeing the birds.

"I am," called Rabbi Zusya.

The innkeeper was so angry that he picked up a broom and chased after Rabbi Zusya. He swung at him once and then twice. Rabbi Zusya managed to stay just out of reach as he fled for his life. Through the front door he ran and out into the dark countryside. He did not stop running until he had gotten very far away from the innkeeper and his broom.

Now he had no place to stay for the night. He had lost the money he used to pay for his room at the inn. No matter! Rabbi Zusya slept very soundly under the stars that night. He did not mind the cold ground nor the few coins he had lost during the night's escapade. As he closed his eyes, he remembered a teaching from the Midrash: "Even the fleas, gnats, and flies are part of God's creation." So, those birds were just as much a part of God's creation as the Jewish prisoners. Rabbi Zusya fell asleep, satisfied that he had fulfilled the mitzvah of freeing the captives.

(Adapted from chasidic lore)

Jewish tradition considers life to be sacred; that means all life. Thus, the rabbis teach us that God stopped the angels and the Israelites from celebrating after the Egyptians had drowned in the Red Sea. "What is there to celebrate?" asks God. "The Egyptians are My children, too, and they have drowned." The deaths of even those who had enslaved and persecuted other human beings did not cause God to rejoice. What does this teach us about the Jewish view of the value of life?

What do you think Rabbi Zusya would have said if someone had asked him why he risked getting hurt to free those birds? What is the lesson Rabbi Zusya is teaching us by setting the birds free? Did Rabbi Zusya fulfill the mitzvah of setting free the captives by letting the birds out of their cage?

The Lord called to him [Moses] from the mountain, saying, "Thus shall you say to the house of Jacob and declare to the children of Israel: 'You have seen what I did to the Egyptians, how I bore you on eagles' wings and brought you to Me. Now then, if you will obey Me faithfully and keep My covenant, you shall be My treasured possession among all the peoples. . . .'" All the people answered as one, saying, "All that the Lord has spoken we will do!"

Exodus 19:3–5,8

The Fox and the Fishes

WHEN THE LAND OF JUDEA was ruled by the Romans who forbade the Jews to teach and study Torah, there lived a great rabbi whose name was Akiva. Once, when Akiva was teaching Torah secretly to a group of students, a young boy burst into the cave where the class was meeting.

"Rabbi Akiva, Rabbi Akiva," he gasped, out of breath from his dash up the hills to the cave, "the Roman soldiers are not far. They are searching the hills for Jewish rebels. You must escape. You must leave before it's too late."

Rabbi Akiva paused in his lesson and motioned for two of his students to bring some water to the young boy who had collapsed from exhaustion. He bent over the youth and took his head in his old, rugged hands.

"Leave? Escape to where? Isn't the whole world filled with

danger and threats to the survival of every Jew?" Akiva paused and looked into the eyes of the boy. He spoke softly.

"I am safer here than anywhere else, and so are you."

The boy opened his eyes wide in disbelief. He could not understand what Akiva had just said. His confusion was clearly etched on his young face and Akiva saw it.

"I see you do not quite understand. Let me tell you this story and perhaps that will make my point for me."

Shuali, the fox, was clever. At least he thought so. But right now, he was hungry. He had not eaten in days.

"Fish," he said, "I think I will have fish tonight."

So, he left the woods to walk along the banks of the stream and wait for his dinner to swim by. Ah, the life of a fox! All he needs to do is decide upon what he wants and then, in a flash, a plan appears in his mind's eye.

"If I sit here in the sun and enjoy the cool breeze, my patience will be rewarded with a wonderful, fresh fish dinner."

Didn't I tell you that Shuali was clever. You don't believe that his plan will work, do you? Well, look up ahead and see the school of fish swimming downsteam towards our hungry friend.

"Gefilte fish," said Shuali. "I am not in the mood for gefilte fish tonight. Go on, swim by and bring on the other fish."

Moments later, a flying fish flew by. Shuali just watched and turned his attention back to the stream.

"Imagine what that would feel like in my stomach, flying around all night as I tried to sleep. Why, I would have indigestion all night long."

More time passed and Shuali was growing hungrier. Just then he looked up and began licking his lips. That was exactly what he had in mind.

"Mackerel," he cried. "Holy mackerel!"

"We're not mackerel," replied one of the fish that had heard Shuali shout. "We're pike. Next time get it right! We are certainly prettier than any mackerel you've ever seen."

"Yes, I see," replied Shuali in his most apologetic tone. He was staring at a fabulous fish dinner and he was not about to let them get away.

"Please forgive me," apologized Shuali. "You are much prettier than any mackerel. Would you come closer so that I can see just how beautiful you are."

Shuali came down to the side of the stream, but not too close because he did not want to frighten these fish and lose his chance to snatch them up.

The fish came a bit closer, but not too close.

"Yes, I think I see the difference between you and the mackerel. But I am getting older and need a better view. Come just a bit closer," asked Shuali in a very friendly and innocent voice.

The fish came a bit closer, but still not too close. Shuali realized that he would never get to eat at this rate. It was time for another idea. Like a flash, it came to our clever friend or, should we say, clever fiend.

"How do you swim so happily and easily when such danger awaits you?" asked Shuali.

"What do you mean?" the fish wanted to know. She stopped swimming around with her friends and lifted her head out of the water.

"Haven't you heard? There is a pack of hunters waiting downstream to catch all the fish that come their way. You are fish, aren't you?"

"Of course we are! What do we look like to you?"

"Well," said Shuali, "if I were a fish I would look to escape from the clutches of those hunters."

"What shall we do, what shall we do?" cried the fish as they panicked, swimming in circles and bumping into one another.

"If you would like," said Shuali, "I can save you. But you must come out of the water and hop on my back. I know of another stream, across the woods. I'll bring you there and then you can go along on your way."

The fish stopped swimming in circles and huddled together to talk over Shuali's offer. Meanwhile, Shuali watched and licked his lips. He was thinking about how tasty these fish would be.

Then, the fish turned to Shuali and the leader moved forward, close but not too close to the banks of the stream. She picked her head out of the water and spoke: "You are supposed to be the cleverest of creatures, but you are really the most foolish. If we come with you, you will eat us. If we leave the water, we will die. So, though there may be danger ahead, our chances of survival are best if we stay where we belong."

Rabbi Akiva finished speaking and looked up at the boy who had come to warn him of the danger which lay ahead.

"You see, I am a Jew and I live in the world of Torah. My chances of survival are best if I stay in the world where I belong."

(Adapted from the Talmud)

The covenant at Sinai was established between God and all the people of Israel. Our part of the agreement was a vow to make the teachings of Torah the guiding spirit of our lives. More than simply rules and regulations, it touched the essence of our existence. As Hillel said: "The more Torah, the more life." Our story relates an episode in the life of the great sage, Akiva. Faced with the possibility of death if he insists on teaching Torah, Akiva insists that Torah is as essential to our existence as water is to the life of a fish. He is ready to die rather than give up Torah.

There have been many other such examples in the annals of our people. What is the greatest possession you ever sacrificed? Why did you make such a sacrifice? Could you imagine being in the position of Akiva? What would you have done? Why was Torah so important to Akiva? What is special for you about the Torah and being Jewish?

· MISHPATIM ·

When a man gives money or goods to another for safekeeping, and they are stolen from the man's house—if the thief is caught, he shall pay double.   Exodus 22:6

A Trustworthy Friend

MORE THAN SIX HUNDRED YEARS AGO, there lived a king named Philip. He issued a decree that told all Jews in his kingdom to leave within two days or be killed. So, all the Jews of France packed whatever they could carry, as quickly as they could, and started to walk up any roads that would take them out of the country.

Simon and his family were among the Jews who had to leave their homeland. Simon had grown up in his home. His mother had grown up in it before him. His wife, Sarah, had grown up in that same town and her family had lived there for hundreds of years. King Philip had given them a couple of days to sell whatever they could to whomever would buy it. How does a family like Simon's pack everything it has on a small cart or in bags that can be carried for weeks until a new home can be found in a new land? What do you take and what do you leave behind?

Simon was a trader who bought and sold precious gems. He was afraid to bring them with him because the king's soldiers might steal them. So, Simon wrapped them up in a clean cloth which was plain and well-worn. That way, they would not attract attention. He decided to give them to his neighbor, Claude, who was Christian and did not have to leave. Simon had known Claude all his life. They had played together as children. Although he was not Jewish, Claude was Simon's closest friend.

"Someday, the decree will be revoked," Simon said when he brought the precious package to Claude. "When that day comes, Sarah and I will return and our gems will be safe."

Many years passed. Simon and Sarah had found another home. Yet, not a day went by during which they did not pray to return to France.

Finally, it happened. King Philip died and his son took over the throne. He announced that all Jews that had been banished from France would be allowed to return to their homes.

Simon and Sarah could not believe it. Their prayers had been answered. Still, there was one question that remained unanswered. Would Claude have protected the gems or would he have sold them?

After many weeks of walking, Simon and Sarah had reached the little town which had been home to them and their families for so many years. They went directly to Claude to ask for the gems.

"For years I have prayed for your return," said Claude, as he embraced them both. "Didn't you once teach me, Simon, that in your Jewish tradition there is a saying, 'A good friend is a tower of strength: to find one is to find a treasure'? If I had sacrificed your friendship for the price of these gems, I would have lost a treasure far more valuable to me."

Claude walked to the middle of the room and dug up the ground underneath his bed. There was the ragged cloth in which Simon had placed his gems so many years before.

The two friends embraced and rejoiced over the great treasure they possessed.

(Adapted from a Yiddish legend)

Ibn Gabirol once said: "The meek becomes known in anger, the hero in war, and a friend in time of need." The routine of our daily lives brings us together with many acquaintances. The trials of extraordinary times show us the few who are true friends. Like our Torah portion, Simon and his family had to entrust a very precious possession to someone else. They turned to a man named Claude whom Simon had known since childhood. Would he be the friend they sought in a time of real need?

What does it mean to be a friend? What kinds of things do friends do for each other? Are there any examples of friendship in the Bible? What kinds of things did these friends do for each other? Do you think you could have done what Claude did? Recall a time when you helped a friend who really needed you.

· TERUMAH ·

And let them make Me a sanctuary that I may dwell among
them.   Exodus 25:8

-->> <<--

There's Always a Right and a Left

I<small>T WAS SHORTLY AFTER</small> the Great Moon Disaster. The Helmites
were desperate—they could stand their poverty no longer. They
crowded the square, calling for bread. Now the younger and
bolder ones cried out against Gimpel, demanding that he sell
the mill and bring prosperity back to Helm.

And, for once, Gimpel, the wisest man in Helm, didn't have
an idea in his head. He stood in the Town Hall and listened to
their cries and couldn't think of a thing. "Maybe it's because
my stomach is empty too," he worriedly remarked to himself.
Then it was that he called the young men to him and said at
last: "Fetch the miller! Let us sell him the mill!"

The neighboring miller came quickly, counted out his gold,
and the mill was his. In no time at all, he had turned it into a
windmill. And all was well in Helm again.

Once more, herring appeared on the Helmite's table instead
of in his dreams. The menfolk worked in the fields, the women
gossiped in the marketplace, the children played when they didn't
fight, and the old folks argued whether it would rain today or
tomorrow. All was well in Helm again.

Only the rabbi wasn't satisfied. One fine Sabbath, when the
synagogue was packed with people, he announced that a town
meeting would be held that night. Immediately after evening services, the Helmites gathered to hear what the rabbi had to say.

"Citizens of Helm!" he began. "God has blessed us and life is good. There is plenty of bread and even herring. We really want for nothing, but I tell you, something is wrong." A puzzled clamor arose, whereupon the rabbi continued.

"Helmites, we must build a new synagogue."

"What's wrong with the old one?" came a cry.

"The roof leaks, the walls are cracked, and the paint is peeling," replied the rabbi quickly.

"Then why not repair it?" asked a Helmite.

"What do you think we are," retorted the rabbi, "paupers from Pultusk?"

"The rabbi's right!" shouted the Helmites. "Helm must have a new synagogue!"

At the break of dawn the very next day, the Helmites met in the forest on the mountaintop. There they set to work chopping down trees for their new synagogue. Seizing saws and axes, they fell upon the tall pines and the great oaks and soon sparks were flying all over the place. Tree after tree was felled by the industrious Helmites and, within no time at all, almost the entire forest had been turned into logs, stripped clean—trimmed of branches, peeled of bark, and ready to be carried down the mountain.

Laboriously, with much grunting and more groaning, the Helmites carried the logs down into the valley, twelve men for each of the smaller logs and twenty men for the larger ones. Finally, only one great oak log was left, so huge they could not budge it from the spot though they used as many men as could squeeze together along the length of it. It was such a beautiful log, however, they wouldn't think of abandoning it and so they sat there, trying to figure out what to do.

They sat and sat until along came Berel the Beadle who was running an errand for the rabbi. When he learned of their plight, he thought for a while, scratched the back of his head, and then suggested, "The log is round, isn't it? Round objects are rolled downhill, not carried. Don't you remember how you rolled me down the hill in the millstone? Why not roll it down?"

Though they had little respect for Berel's wisdom, they remembered that what he said was true. In fact, they were even a little shocked that they hadn't thought of it themselves—they should have remembered how the millstones rolled down the hill, especially the one with Berel sticking out of it. True, round objects must be rolled downhill, not carried.

Whereupon the Helmites trudged down into the valley, painfully dragged all the logs back up the mountain one by one, and then carefully rolled them down again. Not forgetting the great, thick, heavy log of oak, too—not the Helmites.

When Gimpel, who was supervising the building of the synagogue, as he supervised everything in Helm, heard that all the logs were down in the valley, he went out to see how the work was getting on. He was amazed to find the Helmites standing about in little groups, bickering, quarreling, and doing nothing.

"Helmites, is this how you do God's work? Is this the way to build a synagogue—with your tongues?" demanded Gimpel.

"Well," mumbled one of the Helmites, "we were about to carry the logs into the courtyard of the new synagogue but we found out that each log has two ends, a left end and a right end."

"Well, and what's wrong with that?" asked Gimpel. "That's how it is with logs—they always have left and right ends."

"We know that," replied the Helmite. "But what's bothering us is who should go first. Those carrying the right end say that *they* should go first, yet those carrying the left insist that *they* should."

"Excellent arguments," observed Gimpel. "They must be pondered."

So he pondered for a while. Took a pinch of snuff. Sneezed. And even coughed for good measure. Then his eyes brightened and his head cleared.

"I know what! cut off the right end of the log, then only the left end will remain."

Satisfied, two Helmites sawed off the right end of a log and threw it away. Then six men on one side and six men on the other seized the log and began carrying it into the courtyard. They reached the entrance when, lo and behold, they noticed that the log still had two ends, a right and a left. Again the same problem—which end should go in first?

The Helmites dropped the log, returned to Gimpel, and said: "The log still has two ends and we still can't decide who should go in first."

Declared Gimpel: "If the right-enders are so stubborn, then slice off the left end and let's be done with it. No more rights and no more lefts."

And so it was done. But, whether you believe it or not, the

log still persisted in having two ends. No matter how much they cut off from one side or the other, there still remained a left and a right. By now Gimpel lost patience and commanded sternly: "Carry the logs sideways—and let no one, either right or left, complain."

The Helmites lifted the logs and began carrying them sideways, but now a new problem arose—the street was too narrow.

Said Gimpel, "Now this concerns everybody. Let us call a town meeting."

And the wisest men in all Helm sat for seven nights and seven days and thought. When so many sages think for so long, they should think up something really clever. On the eighth day they issued the following proclamation:

> It has come to our attention that no matter how much one cuts a log, it still has two ends—a left and a right—therefore, the logs must be carried sideways. It has also come to our attention that the street is too narrow. Let us, then, tear down the houses on both sides of the street as far as the synagogue.

And that is what the Helmites did. They tore down the houses on both sides of the street. Then, without further ado, they carried the logs sideways right into the courtyard of the new synagogue.

The Helmites set to work building their new synagogue. They worked with zeal and, in no time at all, the walls were up and there was the roof, its bright red shingles proudly gleaming in the sun. So far, so good. No quarrels, not even a cross word. That is, sad to relate, until it came to laying the floor. Then the fur began to fly. Helm was split in two, those in favor of smooth boards and those against. Never was there such a commotion in Helm!

And what was it all about? Nothing trivial, I assure you, for, after all, this was Helm and not Shedlitz or some other town full of simpletons. As everyone knows, on that most solemn fast day known as Yom Kippur, Jews remove their shoes in synagogue and pray in their stockinged feet. Now, if the floor boards were not planed smooth, some Helmite might get a splinter in the foot, a splinter leads to a sore foot, a sore foot makes one limp, limping often causes one to fall and break one's neck—and, reader, do you want a broken neck?

The opposition in Helm argued in this fashion: True, there is some danger if the boards are not planed, but there is even greaer peril if the floor is too smooth. For, on Simchas Torah, which is a very joyous holiday, Jews dance about the synagogue with the Holy Torah in their arms. On a planed floor, they'd naturally slip and fall. Then all of Helm would have to fast and mourn for forty days and forty nights because the Holy Torah had been dropped.

Gimpel carefully weighed the arguments, decided that both sides were right, and rendered the following solution which was not without true Helmite wisdom:

> The boards must indeed be smooth because the danger of splinters on Yom Kippur is great; but let only one side be planed, then lay the smooth, planed side face downwards with the rough side up so that, when the Helmites dance on Simchas Torah, they won't slip and fall with the Holy Torah in their arms.

And so it was done. The new synagogue was completed and Helm celebrated.

(*From Solomon Simon,* The Wise Men of Helm
and Their Merry Tales, *New York: Behrman
House, 1942, reprinted by permission*)

Our story is one of the great tales from the wonderful treasury of Helm stories. We laugh when we read of the adventures of these simpletons. Laughter is good. It is important. These stories have delighted children and adults for years. Our tale talks of the time when the Helmites decided to build a new synagogue for their town. Moses, too, must have met with extraordinary circumstances in his effort to guide the Israelites in their construction of the desert sanctuary.

What kind of sanctuary would you design for a group of Jews wandering in a desert? How would you get the materials you needed? The Helmites had their own plans for building their synagogue. Why do you think it was so important for them to have a new synagogue? What kind of building is a synagogue? We Jews have had synagogues for many years. Throughout our travels around this world we have made sure we had a synagogue. According to a folk saying: "If there were only two Jews left in the world, one would summon the other to the synagogue—and he would go." When was your synagogue built? Who built it? What is the name of your synagogue? What does the name mean? If you could choose a name for a synagogue, what would it be?

· TETZAVEH ·

You shall further instruct the Israelites to bring you clear oil of beaten olives for lighting, for kindling lamps regularly. Aaron and his sons shall set them up in the Tent of Meeting, outside the curtain which is over the Pact, [to burn] from evening to morning before the Lord. It shall be a due from the Israelites for all time, throughout the ages.

Exodus 27:20–21

➳➳➳ ⫷⫷⫷

Torah Is the Best Merchandise

Rabbi Simcha, known as the pious one, was off on a journey. It was his task in life to teach in the small communities of the vast Ottoman Empire, in the days of Sultan Bejazet II. Life was not easy for Rabbi Simcha. He was always traveling from one town to the next. He had no real home and endured an endless succession of small towns, one after the other, after the other.

As he climbed into the carriage that would bring him to Smyrna he wedged himself in among the other passengers. There was a very large man, with a long black beard and two huge bags on his lap. He took up the whole seat across from where Rabbi Simcha squeezed himself into a space. Next to him sat a woman with a bird cage, covered with a richly embroidered, crimson, silk cloth. Both traveling companions looked at the rabbi and smiled weakly.

"This is none of my business, I know," said the huge man,

"but I think you would be much better off if you brought your bags inside the carriage. Even if they are secured tightly to the baggage rack, there is always the chance that the rough roads will jostle them right off the carriage. Then where would you be! Yes, take my advice and you will do well. Everyone who takes my advice does well."

"Your words do sound wise to my ears," replied Rabbi Simcha, "but they are wasted on me. I have no bags, no luggage, no belongings except one very special treasure which I keep hidden in a special place."

"What! You have no luggage, no belongings!" exclaimed the woman. She could not believe her ears. "I don't know what I would do if I did not have my beautiful clothes and jewelry. Don't you find them exquisite?" she asked Rabbi Simcha. And, as he opened his mouth to respond, she went right on speaking, leaving Rabbi Simcha's mouth wide open so that a fly found its way inside and back out again.

"Why, if I did not have my prize bird, Tzip Tzip, I . . . I . . . don't know what I would do. She is the most beautiful creature you have ever seen, isn't she?" Again the rabbi opened his mouth to respond and was left with a mouthful of fresh air because once more she continued without waiting for him to answer. "I own only beautiful things, don't you agree?"

This time, Rabbi Simcha smiled his response. He was not about to risk eating flies for lunch again.

"You think that fancy pigeon is something special," challenged the huge man across the carriage. "Just take a look at the stones I have here in this bag. Precious stones from all over the Mediterranean." And he opened the bag just enough for the sparkle of the gems to blind the rabbi with their brilliance.

For hour upon hour, Rabbi Simcha sat and listened to his travel companions. Listening was all he could do, for they never stopped talking long enough for him to have a chance to get in a word of his own.

Eventually, the nonstop chatter exhausted them all and they dozed off. The abrupt halt of the carriage threw them out of their seats and awakened them rather rudely. Tzip Tzip was dashed against the side of her cage and feathers flew this way and that. The man had fallen forward and onto the lap of Rabbi Simcha, nearly breaking his legs from the burden of the flying weight. The lady next to Rabbi Simcha was all in a tither, crying about poor Tzip Tzip and fussing about her once beautiful hat that now sat crushed and misshapen on her head, after smashing back against the wall of the carriage.

They were being robbed. Everything was taken: the man's bags of gems; the woman's coat and hat; and even Tzip Tzip was removed and wisked away by the robbers.

His travel companions were inconsolable with grief, and Rabbi Simcha spent the rest of the trip trying to make them feel better. As long as he could not bring back the items they had lost, Rabbi Simcha found his neighbors unwilling to listen to anything he had to say.

"I am ruined!" cried the man. "I am nothing without my gems."

"Tzip Tzip, my beautiful Tzip Tzip! My fur, my hat, my jewels! What will I do? My life is over," sobbed the woman.

Finally, they arrived in Smyrna. They departed the carriage and went on their own separate ways. The next day, the man with the gems was wandering the streets of Smyrna, contemplating his fate, when he overheard some people talking very excitedly about a great visitor who had come to town.

"Maybe, this great sage can advise me about how I can restore my wealth and recover my gems," thought the man. So, he headed over to the marketplace and waited to meet the special visitor.

It was very crowded and hard to see. Suddenly, the crowd began to part down the middle to make way for the guest of honor. When the part reached him, the man could not believe his eyes. It was none other than Rabbi Simcha.

Immediately, the rabbi noticed his carriage neighbor and approached him.

"All during our trip you bragged of your wealth and of your reputation. Yet, when we were robbed, your fame was stolen as well. My treasure was the knowledge of Torah which I keep here inside. When gems are stolen, when silver tarnishes, when beauty fades away, my treasure will remain as brilliant and valuable as ever."

Then, Rabbi Simcha turned to the crowd which had assembled to hear him teach.

There is a folk saying that teaches: "Every Jew must light a *ner tamid* in his own heart." What kind of light must we keep burning within us? The light of Torah. Torah has often been compared to a light. "Torah is light." (*Proverbs* 6:23) When we hear a little voice within us whispering, "Remember you were a stranger once in the land of Egypt," and reach out to help someone we may not know, we are keeping the lamp of Torah kindling inside. When we hear that voice reminding us to keep the Sabbath and we endeavor to do so, we are taking care of that flame. The point of our story is that Rabbi Simcha has a gift that cannot be taken away or stolen like the prized possessions of his travel companions. Once the teachings of the Torah get inside you, they can never be taken away.

Why were the thieves unable to steal the Torah from Rabbi Simcha? Which teachings from the Torah do you keep inside? Our tradition teaches us: "Torah should lead to good deeds." What do you think this means?

· KI TISA ·

And the Lord spoke to Moses, saying: Speak to the Israelite people and say: Nevertheless, you must keep My sabbaths, for this is a sign between Me and you throughout the ages, that you may know that I the Lord have consecrated you. You shall keep the sabbath, for it is holy for you.

Exodus 31:12–14

→)) ((←

A Shabbat Miracle

Yitzhak and his wife Rebecca were poor. "Poverty is no disgrace, but it is no great honor either." Each day brought its difficulties. Would Yitzhak have enough books to bind to make a living? Would the patches in the roof hold to keep the winter wind outside the house rather than grant it entrance like an unwanted relative? Would there be enough scraps of food left over from the night before for Rebecca to eke out one more day of stew? Would the cow have enough to eat so that she might give milk? So Yitzhak and Rebecca faced each new day like Christopher Columbus. They woke up and wondered if this was the day they would fall off the face of the earth or if they would make it through to face yet another morning, tomorrow. They had *tsores*. Poor people have *tsores*, rich people "face challenges."

This morning was Friday. Tonight Shabbat would arrive. Did Yitzhak have a good enough week to afford the candles, the wine, the chalah, the chicken, and other food? The emptiness in his stomach was as deep as a bottomless pit. There was his answer!

"Rebecca, you will need to be very clever today to pull together enough from here and enough from there to make this house ready for *Shabbes*."

75

"What's wrong all of a sudden," asked Rebecca with a start. "You think that today is such an exception. Tonight, when you get home from *shul,* you will find *Shabbes* has chosen this house as the most fitting place for a personal visit. The *Shechinah* herself will be all dressed up and waiting for you. Don't trip over her gown when you come in the door!"

"*Tsores* brings its own brand of humor," thought Yitzhak as he started out for his store. "It seems warmer outside than inside." And he was on his way.

Rebecca really did not know what she was going to do to prepare their house for Shabbat. This week, things truly were worse than they had ever been before. But her heart was full of the spirit of Shabbat and she began to sing as she sat down to clean the two tarnished candlesticks that sat all week on top of the mantle, waiting to be placed in the center of the dinner table where they would shine, bringing light and joy.

Since there was less food than usual to cook, Rebecca had more time for cleaning. She hummed as she swept, swinging the broom to the rhythm of the *niggun.* The music moved her and inspired her every action. Faster and faster she swept, dancing as she went. In her joy, she even decided to move the old trunk that stood on the floor by the wall. It functioned as a kind of table, with a faded cloth draped over its top. She could not recall the last time she had opened it. They owned almost nothing of real value, save for the candlesticks, a few of Yitzhak's books, and her wedding dress.

How she had looked that night when she stood under the *chupah* with Yitzhak! She had a glow about her that kindled the stars in the sky. Although her knees shook through the whole ceremony, no one could tell because her smile was radiant and her white, silk wedding dress was the kind of garment only an angel would wear.

Rebecca removed the cloth from atop the beaten and battered trunk and raised the lid slowly. She smelled the stale air and saw the layer of dust that had blanketed the inner walls of the trunk along with all that rested inside, including her wedding gown. Carefully, she picked it up and unfolded it. With trembling hands she held it up against her and gazed into the mirror. At that moment, she was transformed into that same angel that had stood at Yitzhak's side all those years ago. There was something magical about that gown. She did not understand its powers—although there was no denying its effect.

Rebecca stood before the mirror for a long moment. Shabbat! The thought of Shabbat appeared in her mind, and she knew that there was still much to do to get their house ready to receive Shabbat when she would come to visit in a few hours. As she folded her gown, something caught her eye. It was a glimmer of light coming from inside the trunk. Something in there was reflecting what little sunlight shone through the ice-covered windows.

There, on the bottom of that trunk, were seven shining buttons. They were brilliant and as yellow as the sun.

"Could they have been underneath my gown all these years?" thought Rebecca. "Where did they come from?"

Despite her curiosity, her excitement won the moment and moved her to run from the house all the way to Perchik, the pawnbroker.

"Hu, ha!" cried Perchik when he took a look at the gold buttons in Rebecca's trembling hand. "That's quite a *metsiah* you've got there." He counted out a huge sum of coins which he put into a velvet bag.

Rebecca could not believe it. Never had she seen so much money before! She pinched herself until she turned black and blue. She could not bear to think she was dreaming. If she were dreaming, then she did not wish to wake up, ever.

As she ran giddily down the street, she came across a beggar. "Here," she said as she handed him a coin. "*Gut Shabbes!*"

"Yitzhak and I observed the mitzvah of *tzedakah* when we were poor. How much the more should we fulfill it now that we have a few coins in our pocket."

When Yitzhak returned home from *shul* that night, he could not believe his eyes. There before him was a picture of Shabbat one might expect only in the world to come. The rickety dinner table was covered with the most beautiful white, embroidered cloth. There was a chalah as big and puffy as any he had ever seen. Even the candlesticks, the old tarnished candlesticks, were gleaming as they did when he and Rebecca had used them for the first time on the first Shabbat after they had married. The kiddush cup was full of wine, and the whole house was filled with the aroma of the most mouthwatering chicken soup his nostrils had ever known. But, more than all this, there was Rebecca. She stood behind the dancing candlelight, her face reflecting its glow. Never had she seemed more beautiful.

Yitzhak was overcome with love and the extra soul which fills our beings on Shabbat. He took Rebecca by her hands and they danced around the room, humming and singing *zemirot*. They laughed and celebrated all through that Shabbat and on into the next week.

So great was their joy that night that the Ba'al Shem Tov was moved by the force of their gladness to stop at three different times during his own Shabbat meal. When Yitzhak and Rebecca danced and sang around their room, the simple and complete joy in their souls was felt within the soul of the revered Ba'al Shem Tov himself. And so he laughed, and he laughed, and then he cried with joy. It is said that Shabbat brings to our lives a foretaste of the world to come. That night, the world to come and our world were one and the same.

(Adapted from chasidic folklore)

"He who makes the Sabbath a delight shall have the wishes of his heart fulfilled." (*Shabbat* 118a) In "A Shabbat Miracle," Yitzhak and Rebecca discover how the joy of the Sabbath can make dreams come true.

What kinds of things did Yitzhak and Rebecca do to make the Sabbath special? What kinds of things do you do to make it just as special in your home? Why did Rebecca stop to give money to the beggar on the street? Did you know that setting aside *tzedakah* on the Sabbath is a very old Jewish custom?

· VAYAKHEL/PEKUDE ·

When Moses had finished the work, the cloud covered the Tent of Meeting, and the Presence of the Lord filled the Tabernacle.   Exodus 40:33–34

⤜⤛

No Room for the BeSHT

It was erev Yom Kippur. This was a magical night, a special night—the holiest night of the year. The Ba'al Shem Tov, whom many called the BeSHT from the initial letters of his name, was on his way to the *shtibl* to hear the chanting of *Kol Nidre*.

The sun had begun to set in the sky. Huge streaks of red and orange and purple radiated throughout the sky. Three stars were faintly visible overhead. Autumn leaves had fallen from the trees and had turned dry and brittle on the ground. They crunched and crumbled under the BeSHT's feet as he made his way through the forest.

He was very deep in thought, reviewing in his mind the way he had behaved during the past year. He recalled how he helped some people, but he also realized that there were others he could have helped more. He remembered some harsh words he spoke in moments of anger and regretted them. He was reminded of people he may have hurt with comments or opinions. During this last month of Elul, he had tried to ask forgiveness from those whom he had offended. As well, he had spent many hours considering how he could become a better person in the year to come. Now, most people who knew the Ba'al Shem Tov would not have been able to imagine how such a kind and pious person could become more kind and pious than he was already. But the Ba'al Shem Tov knew that there was room for improvement. He knew that only a very arrogant person could think that he was without fault.

The Ba'al Shem Tov had been so deep in thought that he had not realized that the *shtibl* was only a few yards ahead. As he approached this small, wooden structure, he could see that it was full of people.

When he was within a few feet of the door, he stopped cold in his tracks. A vision had come to him, and he could see nothing else before him save it. The angels in heaven circled around the Divine Throne, covering their ears with their hands, trying to keep from hearing some kinds of sound. What was it that they did not want to hear anymore? Suddenly, the BeSHT could hear what they heard. Sounds of human voices became audible. All kinds of voices, each one more pleading than the other.

"Please, I need to have more customers during this next year!"

Then another voice: "I must make more money next year!"

Then a different voice: "I want more people to like me!"

Then more voices and more voices. Each one asking for something else. And suddenly the BeSHT knew what he was listening to. He knew that he had been given the chance to hear the prayers of the people inside the *shtibl* on their way to heaven. The angels could stand no more of this selfishness on erev Yom Kippur.

The door to the *shtibl* opened and a gust of wind blew through. Papers flew, pages of prayer books turned, and some of the men lost their yarmulkes. All eyes turned to the door where the Ba'al Shem Tov stood. Instead of entering, the BeSHT just stood there. After a few moments, one of the men closest to the door invited the BeSHT to come in.

"I cannot enter," said the BeSHT. "There is no room in here for me."

Everyone looked around. There seemed to be many people inside the little one-room house that served as the *shtibl*. Still, there was enough room for a few more bodies to squeeze in. Strange that the BeSHT would say that there was not enough room for him.

"You have already filled this room to the brim with your selfishness," said the Ba'al Shem Tov. "You are each too filled with yourselves and your own importance and your own needs. You have no room in your thoughts for anyone else. What room have you left for God? There is no room in God's own house for God!"

So, the Ba'al Shem Tov left the *shtibl* and went into the midst of the forest where he spent Yom Kippur.

(Adapted from chasidic folklore)

Vayakhel and *Pekude* are included here as a double portion. Since the Jewish calendar is based on a lunar cycle of 354 days, or 50 weeks a year, we would not be able to read the 54 regular Torah portions unless we paired some of them. *Vayakhel* and *Pekude* are often paired. Later, you will find that *Tazria* and *Metzora* and *Matot* and *Mas'ey* are also paired.

Our story, "No Room for the BeSHT," tells of a particular erev Yom Kippur when the great teacher Israel Ba'al Shem Tov refused to enter a *shtibl* because the selfishness of the worshipers left no room for him or God to enter. Our Torah portion deals with the same theme. It depicts one of many occasions when God's presence descended upon the Tabernacle and suffused it with divinity. Like our ancestors, we are called upon to make our synagogues places where God would want to reside. When we become self-centered, we shut out others from entering our lives and, in the process, we shut out God as well.

What did the Ba'al Shem Tov hear as he walked to the *shtibl*? What did he do when he got to the door of the *shtibl*? What was the reaction of those who were already inside? Why did the Ba'al Shem Tov refuse to enter? Our Torah portion speaks about the presence of God filling the Tabernacle. What did the Ba'al Shem Tov tell us we have to do in order for God's presence to fill our synagogues? What kinds of things can we do when we are at services to follow the Ba'al Shem Tov's teaching?

· VAYIKRA ·

It is a burnt offering, an offering by fire, of pleasing odor
to the Lord.   Leviticus 1:13

→))) (((←

Rabbi Chanina's Gift
of Stone

CHANINA BEN DOSA was a very famous man. His wisdom brought
him students from far and wide, but these were poor students.
You cannot take your reputation to the bank, so Chanina was a
man of wealth in wisdom and reputation only. He owned very
little. His family had very little and often were hungry. Yet, no
one complained for, despite their poverty, they were happy. They
envied no one and lived each day grateful for that which came
their way.

As fall approached, Chanina saw his neighbors preparing to
go to the Temple in Jerusalem. Three times each year, Jews were
to make a pilgrimage to Jerusalem and appear at the Temple
before God. No matter how far away one lived, no matter how
busy one was, everyone was expected to make this journey—
and everyone did.

Each visit to Jerusalem was an occasion to bring an offering
to the priests as a sacrifice to God. Time after time, Chanina
watched as his neighbors presented gifts of great wealth while
he had next to nothing to give. This fall he had even less than
usual to bring.

What would he give? In his despair he walked among the hills
near his home in Arav in the Lower Galilee. As he walked aimlessly,
he came upon a huge stone that seemed to appear before him

from out of nowhere. While it was very large and crude, it had a kind of attraction to it that intrigued Chanina. He looked it over and an idea came to him.

"If I polished it and decorated it, this stone would become a precious stone and a gift worthy of God."

In the weeks preceding the pilgrimage to Jerusalem, Chanina worked hard to clean the stone and polish its surface. When it began to shine, Chanina took a step back to admire its brilliance in the sunlight. It did have a special beauty, which he was uncovering. Carefully, with a hammer and chisel, he etched magnificient designs into its face.

When he had finished, he sat down and admired his work. It was splendid. It was a precious gift from his heart. But how was he ever going to bring it with him to Jerusalem? It was too large and much too heavy for one person to carry. He needed help and set out to ask his neighbors.

Up the road there were five men cutting down trees. Chanina stopped there to ask for help.

"Sure, we will help you," one of the men replied to Chanina. "But it will cost you. How much can you offer us?"

"I have managed to save five gold coins over the years," said Chanina. "You can have it all if you will help me."

"Five gold coins! We would not even consider helping you for anything less than fifty gold coins. If you can get fifty, we are ready to help; if not, go away and bother someone else!"

Chanina knew there was no way for him to get so much money. He walked away, wondering who would help him.

"Excuse me," Chanina looked up to see that five travelers had approached him.

"How strange!" thought Chanina. "I saw no one on the road and now these five strangers stand before me."

"We have come in search of work," said one of the strangers. "If you can tell us who might need some laborers for hire, we will be on our way."

"If it is work you are looking for, I have work for you," said Chanina. "I can promise you that the work is hard enough to satisfy you, but I am not sure the same can be said for the payment."

"Friend, we would work for five gold coins if we could."

When Chanina heard that they would work for five gold coins, he was overjoyed. Immediately he took out the coins from his pocket and paid the men in advance. Then he brought them to where the stone sat and told them how he needed it brought to Jerusalem in time for the festival of Sukot.

The five men surrounded the stone and rolled up their sleeves. One of them motioned for Chanina to come over and join them as they lifted it up from the earth.

As soon as Chanina touched the stone, the Galilean hills vanished and Chanina found himself in the midst of the marketplace—in Jerusalem. There he stood, just outside the gates to the Temple. The stone gleamed as it reflected the setting sun. But the strangers were gone. What had happened? How did he travel all the way to Jerusalem and not remember any of the journey? Where were his helpers? He was confused and disoriented until he put his hand into his pocket and found his coins. All five were still there even though he was certain that he had given them to the strangers before they disappeared.

Then it all became clear. They were not men at all. They were messengers of God, sent to him to show that his precious gift had been accepted from the moment his heart had offered it.

When Chanina returned to Arav, he gave the five coins to his students.

(Adapted from the Midrash)

The Midrash teaches: "Notice that the words 'pleasing odor to the Lord' are used equally in the case of an ox or a sheep or a bird to show you that the big and the little sacrifice are equal before God. . . ." An offering with all sincerity from the heart is worth so much more than a huge but thoughtless contribution from the pocket.

Those who hear our story might be asked why God accepted Chanina's gift. What has this to teach us? What might be the moral of the story? What counts most about giving a gift? What kinds of *tzedakah* can one perform without giving money?

· TZAV ·

Then Moses brought Aaron and his sons forward and washed them with water. He put the tunic on him, girded him with the sash, clothed him with the robe, and put the *ephod* on him, girding him with the decorated band with which he tied it to him. He put the breastpiece on him, and put into the breastpiece the Urim and Thummim. And he set the headdress on his head; and on the headdress, in front, he put the gold frontlet, the holy diadem—as the Lord had commanded Moses.   Leviticus 8:6–9

->>> <<<-

The Stones of the Breastpiece

MOSES ENTERED the Tent of Meeting alone. Moments later, God descended upon the tent in the midst of a cloud. The people had seen this happen dozens of times during the years of their desert wanderings, but they never grew used to it. God stood in the midst of that cloud! What would it be like to be Moses standing inside that tent?

When the cloud rose from the tent and disappeared into the heavens, Moses emerged. Each time Moses encountered God Moses' appearance changed. His eyes sparkled more. His face seemed calm. His hair was streaked with highlights of silver.

"God has commanded us to make special garments for Aaron and his sons so they might serve as our *kohanim,* our priests," Moses announced.

So the people made special priestly garments: robes, coats, sashes, headdresses, and breastpieces. Each garment had its own powers: the coat was used to atone for murder; the sash atoned for theft; the bells on the robes atoned for slander.

But the breastpiece was the most powerful and most special garment of all. It was decorated with twelve precious stones. Each stone was given by one of the twelve tribes of Israel. Each one was a different color and had its own special powers. The tribe of Levi contributed a deep-red stone called a carbuncle. It made the face of those who wore it beam with the light of wisdom and truth. The tribe of Judah donated an exquisite green emerald. It had the power of making its owner victorious in battle. The tribe of Issachar brought a sparkling blue sapphire, which made the one who wore it healthy. Zebulun brought a perfect white pearl, which had the power to bring restfulness. Gad's stone was a clear crystal, which brought its owner courage in battle.

The tribe of Benjamin possessed a very unique and curious stone, a jasper stone. A jasper stone turns red, green, and black, depending upon the moods of the one who wears it. So, if one were angry, the stone turned bright red; if one were sad, it turned black; if one were envious, it turned green.

All these stones, one from each of the twelve tribes of Israel, were set into the breastpieces worn by Aaron and his sons. When all the breastpieces and other garments had been finished, Moses called all the people together in front of the Tent of Meeting.

"My brother Aaron and his sons now have vestments befitting their roles as priests among us," said Moses. "These garments have special powers that will aid our priests in their service of God and us. Remember always that these powers come from God. Without God, the robes are only fabrics and the precious jewels in the breastpiece are only stones."

Moses then turned to Aaron.

"My brother, are you and your sons prepared to dedicate your lives to the fulfillment of God's mitzvot?"

Aaron and his sons nodded and together they said: "We are ready to dedicate our lives to our God and our people."

So Moses took a jar of oil and sprinkled some of it on the Tent of Meeting. Then he approached Aaron and asked him to bow his head. Slowly, he poured some of the oil onto the head of his brother Aaron. You see, this was not just any oil Moses was using. It was a special oil. When it was poured on people or objects, it marked them as holy and set aside for God's service.

Aaron and his sons were no longer just part of the crowd. They were priests. They were special, as the Tent of Meeting was special.

Up above the ceremony hovered a huge white cloud. At the moment Moses annointed Aaron's head with oil, the cloud parted and a ray of golden sunlight shone through. Some say it was a sign from heaven that God was pleased.

(Adapted from the Midrash)

In our Torah portion, Aaron and his sons are ordained to the priesthood. While Moses had assumed the cultic responsibilities up to this point, Aaron and his sons now became the custodians of these rites and rituals. The priesthood, as it was born during the wilderness wandering, would continue to hold sway over our ancestors' sacerdotal activities until the destruction of the Second Temple by the Romans in 70 C.E.. At about that time, the synagogue, which had existed for years, and the ordination of those called "rabbi" began to take center stage in the religious life of our people.

Aaron and his sons had special garments to wear in their service to God. There are garments for us to wear in our service to God. Have you ever worn a talit? There are those who believe that it is possible to find God when you wrap yourself up in a talit. Do you wear a yarmulke (also called a *kipah*) when you go to temple? Some people wear a yarmulke because it reminds them that God is always with them, sitting right above them like the cloud sat above our ancestors when they wandered in the desert. Could this be so? Do you know of any other special garments we Jews wear for holidays and other celebrations?

They brought to the front of the Tent of Meeting the things that Moses had commanded, and the whole community came forward and stood before the Lord. Moses said: "This is what the Lord has commanded that you do, that the Presence of the Lord may appear to you." Then Moses said to Aaron: "Come forward to the altar and sacrifice your sin offering and your burnt offering, making expiation for yourself and for the people; and sacrifice the people's offering and make expiation for them, as the Lord has commanded."   Leviticus 9:5–7

Aaron and the Altar

T HE HEAVENS ROARED with terrible thunder, and then a commanding voice was heard: "Let them build Me a sanctuary so I can dwell among them." Moses understood God's command clearly.

"We must build a sanctuary," said Moses, stroking his beard. "We must have a home for God to visit us wherever we walk in the desert."

But who would Moses choose to construct the special portable temple called a tabernacle? Ah! Moses devised a clever plan to find the one for the job.

"Let us build the Tabernacle," he declared. "First, let us build the Holy Ark to carry God's teachings. Then, let us construct the altar, the menorah, and all the furniture that will go inside. Finally, let us build the sanctuary to surround it all."

"Yes," shouted the people. "We will do it!" And Moses was almost trampled by the people who came running up to him, volunteering to be the one to have the honor of leading the project.

But, from the back of the crowd, there came a loud voice.

"No! No! That is not the way to build God's Tabernacle."

Well, everyone turned around to see who had the nerve to tell Moses that his idea was wrong. As the crowd parted, a huge man with broad shoulders and eyes as black as coal made his way to where Moses stood.

"That's not the way to build the Tabernacle," he declared as he stood before Moses. "The first thing one does is build one's house. Then one worries about what will go inside. So, first we build the sanctuary, and only them should we design the ark and the altar."

Moses smiled. "That is the answer I was waiting to hear. You, Bezalel, shall be the one to build God's Tabernacle."

Each part of the Tabernacle Bezalel built symbolized something very special. For instance, he made the Tabernacle seventy cubits long and seventy cubits wide. Seventy symbolized the number of holy days in the Jewish calendar: fifty-two Sabbaths, seven days of Passover, eight days of Sukot, one day of Shavuot, one day of Yom Kippur, and one day of Rosh Hashanah. Then, he made the altar five cubits long and five cubits wide. Five stood for the five commandments on each of the two tablets Moses had brought down from Mount Sinai.

Bezalel decorated the corners of the altar with four horns made of brass. The horns looked like the horns on the head of a bull. They were large, curved, and pointed. The four horns stood for the four different times that God had promised to rescue and redeem the Israelites.

One day, Aaron walked by Bezalel while he was working on the altar. As soon as Aaron saw the horns Bezalel was making, he remembered that awful time when the Israelites forced him to help them build an idol in the shape of a golden calf. Aaron recalled that day very well. Moses had been on top of Mount Sinai for many days, waiting to receive God's commandments and teachings. When Moses did not come down right away, the people grew worried. They thought Moses was dead. Even though Moses was alive and well and listening to all of God's teachings, the people believed he would never return. They thought God had deserted them. So they turned to Aaron and asked him to build them an idol to protect them. They wanted a huge calf made of pure gold. What could Aaron do? What were his choices?

Aaron knew the people had panicked. He knew they would never listen to him because they were so frightened. So he decided to do what they asked in order to calm them down. He decided to delay them as much as possible so that Moses would return in time to stop them from worshiping an idol.

Aaron remembered the look in Moses' eyes when he came down from the mountain, carrying God's Ten Commandments, and saw the Golden Calf. His eyes blazed like fire, his face turned red with rage, and he smashed the commandments on the ground.

Aaron looked down at the altar Bezalel was building and saw its horns. They looked like the horns on the Golden Calf. The thought of that terrible time made him sweat and shake. He started to cry. Because he could not stand there any longer, he ran away, far away from the Israelite camp.

Bezalel did not understand why Aaron had gotten so upset. So he told Moses what happened. Moses knew he had to find Aaron.

There he was out in the desert, hundreds of yards from the camp. He was sitting on a rock with his head in his hands. He was sobbing.

"Aaron, Bezalel told me what happened," Moses said as he put his arm around his brother. "Why are you so upset?"

Aaron turned around to face his brother. His face was streaked with tears.

"When I saw the horns on the corners of the altar, I was reminded of the horns on the Golden Calf. It made me so sad to think of that day when I helped our people make an idol."

"Aaron," said Moses softly. "God has told me that you did what you thought was best. You tried to keep peace among the people and hold them together. God has forgiven you. In fact, God wants you to have the honor of offering the first sacrifice on the new altar. Bezalel is preparing the fire for the sacrifice right now. Can you see the smoke rising into the sky above our campsite? Let's go back and offer our sacrifice to God."

Aaron felt better to know that God had forgiven him. He returned to the camp with his brother.

Moses gathered all the people together in front of the new altar.

"This is the altar God commanded us to build," he announced. "Step back and watch as my brother, Aaron, has the honor of offering our very first sacrifice."

Aaron stepped in front of the altar. As soon as he did, a huge cloud formed in the sky and hovered over the Israelite camp. When Aaron lifted the sacrifice, the cloud parted and a bright yellow ray of sunlight shone through and illuminated Aaron and the altar. God was pleased. Aaron smiled.

(*Adapted from the Midrash*)

The first time Aaron saw the altar that Bezalel had built he noticed the four horns placed at its four corners. It reminded him of the Golden Calf he had helped the Israelites construct while waiting for Moses to come down from Mount Sinai. The horror of that recollection so terrified him that he ran from the Tabernacle. Rabbinic literature has sought to excuse Aaron for his role in the Golden Calf episode. Some texts explain that Aaron delayed the calf's construction as long as he could, hoping that Moses would descend the mountain in time. Others speak about his participation in the incident as his attempt to maintain peace in the Israelite camp. Our story pursues this rabbinic line of thought. It depicts Moses speaking with Aaron on God's behalf, telling him that God understood what Aaron had done and forgave him.

Why did Moses give the job of building the Tabernacle to Bezalel? What was so great about Bezalel's answer to Moses' question? Why did Aaron run out of the Tabernacle when he saw the horns on the side of the altar? Why does God forgive Aaron for his role in the construction of the Golden Calf? The Tabernacle was seventy cubits by seventy cubits because this symbolized the seventy holy days of the Jewish calendar. What kinds of symbols exist in your temple? For instance, what is the official logo of your temple? What does the logo stand for? Is there any artwork in the sanctuary? What does it stand for? If you could design the ark or a stained-glass window for your sanctuary, what kinds of symbols would you use?

· TAZRIA/METZORA ·

Tazria/Metzora is included here as a double portion. (See the *Vayakhel/Pekude* chapter for an explanation.)

➤➤➤ ⫷⫷⫷

A Wicked Tongue

HUNDREDS AND HUNDREDS of years ago, there lived a man named Shmuel Hanagid. At the time when Shmuel lived in Spain, the Moslems ruled the land and all went well for the Jews. In fact, Shmuel himself was the advisor to the king. Not bad! Wouldn't you agree? Many people wished to hold such a prestigious position, and some wanted it so badly that they were envious of Shmuel. They would insult him behind his back. They would spread rumors around the city of Granada that Shmuel was out to harm the king, that Shmuel gave the king poor advice, or that Shmuel was looking out for the welfare of only Jews and neglecting the rest of the people.

In particular, there was a merchant who sold goods from a little shop just outside the palace walls. He had heard all the rumors about Shmuel, and he believed them all. So he really hated Shmuel and blamed him for everything that went wrong in the city.

Each morning, when Shmuel walked to the palace, he passed by the merchant's shop. As he went by, the merchant would run out of the shop shouting insults and chase him all the way to the palace gates.

One day, Shmuel went out for a walk with the king. On their way, they passed the merchant's shop. As always, as soon as the merchant spotted Shmuel, he rushed out, screaming insults and accusations. He was so angry and full of hatred that he never noticed the king. But the king noticed him.

"Arrest that man," the king called to the guards that accompanied him. "Throw him in jail until I decide what to do with him."

Sitting in his prison cell, the merchant was no longer angry. Instead, he was very frightened. He imagined the king ordering terrible punishments.

"Perhaps, he would even have my tongue cut out," cried the merchant. The more he thought about it, the more sick at heart he became. Tears rolled down his cheeks, and he sat there sobbing for some time.

What was the king going to do?

"Shmuel, my friend, since the insults were directed at you, I will let you command the punishment," said the king.

"If that is the case," replied Shmuel, "I ask you to release the merchant."

"Release him!" The king could not believe what Shmuel had asked. "Why should I release a man that is full of such hatred and that has directed his anger toward you each and every day for so many years?"

"My tradition teaches that one who seeks forgiveness must first learn to forgive. If I were to cut out his tongue, I would only confirm the terrible impression he has of me and give him a reason to hate me all the more. Let him have a reason to respect me that he has learned for himself."

The king did as Shmuel asked. When the merchant was told that Shmuel had requested his release, he was overjoyed. That next day, when Shmuel passed the shop on his way to the palace, the merchant rushed out and began shouting in Shmuel's direction. This time his voice was full of praise and respect, rather than hatred and insult. In fact, the merchant spread the word of Shmuel's wisdom and compassion all over Granada.

Months later, the king spoke with Shmuel about his act of forgiveness.

"Once again, you have advised me well. I wished to have the man's tongue cut out. But you showed me a way to replace his wicked tongue with one of respect. Such is your wisdom and such is my blessing."

(Adapted from folklore)

The rabbis connected the Hebrew expression for slanderer, *motzi ra,* to the word *metzora,* leper. In the *Zohar* we read: "God will accept repentance for all sins except one: giving another a bad name." That makes slander a very serious offense. Often, slander is disseminated behind the back of its target. It is a cowardly and destructive act. In the story, "A Wicked Tongue," Shmuel Hanagid is the victim of a merchant's slander. Yet, when the opportunity arises for Shmuel to realize vengeance against his slanderer, he forgives the man. What a difficult thing to do!

If someone slandered you, would you be as forgiving as Shmuel? Do you agree with Shmuel's decision? Have you ever spread gossip about someone else? Why? How did the object of your slander feel when that person found out? Have you ever been the subject of gossip or slander? How have you felt? Did you handle it as Shmuel did?

· ACHARE MOT ·

And this shall be to you a law for all time: In the seventh
month, on the tenth day of the month, you shall practice
self-denial; and you shall do no manner of work, neither
the citizen nor the alien who resides among you. For on
this day atonement shall be made for you to cleanse you
of all your sins; you shall be clean before the Lord.

Leviticus 16:29–30

The Tears of Repentance Are the Purest Prayer

THE RABBI wrapped himself in his talit. Now he was all alone.
He could no longer see nor hear his congregation. It was *Ne'ilah*
and the Day of Atonement was drawing to a close. Outside, the
sun was setting. Soon the fast would be broken. Would his prayers
and the prayers of those who stood with him in *shul* be heard in
the highest heaven? Would they all be inscribed in the Book of
Life for a good and sweet year? The rabbi wished to know these
things and, so, he sought out God for just a very few seconds
of precious conversation. Sure, he knew that there were many
others around the world who were seeking God's attention at
this very moment. But . . .

Then, as in a vision, God's response came to the rabbi: If Tam
would pray on behalf of the community, all prayers would be
accepted on high—Tam, the same Tam who always sat in the
very back of the *shul,* without a *machzor* or a *siddur* at anytime,
because he knew neither how to read nor how to recite the proper
prayers.

The rabbi could not believe it. Tam! Not those men who paid

the highest price for a seat near the Eastern Wall; not those who spoke loudest at the rabbi's *shiurim;* not those who had the nicest *kipot* or *talitot.* But Tam!

At once the vision disappeared, and the rabbi found himself alone again enveloped by his talit.

He looked out to his congregation and raised his arms into the air. All stopped. There was silence and everyone looked at the rabbi.

"Bring Tam to the *bimah,*" he whispered. It was so quiet in the *shul* that everyone could hear what the rabbi had said.

"Bring Tam to the *bimah?*" this one whispered to the next. "Why Tam? What is going on here?"

Tam was shocked to hear his name called, especially at this moment during the most sacred service of the year. He had heard his name called, but he could not move his feet. His limbs had become paralyzed by the very awe of the moment. He was aware that all eyes were locked on him. "What could the rabbi possibly want with me?" he thought.

Two men appeared at his side, and they brought Tam before the rabbi. The rabbi put his hands on Tam's shoulders and said: "God has asked that you pray on behalf of our whole community. We await your prayer."

"But, but . . ." stammered Tam. "Everyone knows that I do not know the words of prayer. I cannot read the words. How can I possibly do what you have asked?"

"Tam," said the rabbi, softly and with great kindness. "God has called upon you. Respond to that call in your own way. That is all God asks."

Tam looked into the rabbi's eyes and found strength.

"I will pray as I know how." he said. "But, first, you must give me a moment to get my prayer."

The rabbi did not know what Tam meant. How does one go to get a prayer? But he nodded his approval, and Tam rushed from the *shul.* A great cry went up among the congregation.

"What is going on?" "We demand to know what is happening!"

But the rabbi remained silent as he awaited Tam's return.

After quite a while, Tam returned carrying a plain, clay pitcher. He ascended the *bimah* and stood before the open ark. Holding the pitcher before him, Tam spoke in a quivering, secret-kind of voice: "*Ribono shel olam,* Ruler of the universe, I am not the wisest scholar in the community. I do not know the words to most of the prayers. But, when I pray to You, the words I choose come straight from my heart. At this holiest of moments, I have brought You the most pious gift I own. Here in this pitcher are the tears that I have shed when I sit late at night and think about my wife and children who go to bed each night hungry and do not own even a special dress or shirt for Shabbat. When I think of how much I love them and how much I cannot give them, I weep for hours on end. Here are my tears, they say much more than I can. All I can do is pray that no one else in this community ever will have the reason to cry as I do."

At that moment, the rabbi closed the curtains to the ark. He turned to Tam and said: "Never have I heard such eloquence nor such true piety. It is because of you that God has accepted our prayers. You are the one who should bless this community now as the Day of Atonement ends, not I."

Tam could not believe the honor the rabbi was giving him. He swallowed hard and lifted his hands. With arms outstretched and his heart in his throat, Tam blessed the congregation. He remembered a prayer his wife always said when important things happened in their lives.

Baruch Atah, Adonai Elohenu, Melech ha'olam, shehecheyanu vekiyemanu vehigianu lazeman hazeh.

Blessed are You, O Lord our God, Source of all life, for You have given us the gift of life, given us our health, and granted us the happiness of sharing this wonderful moment together. Amen.

The community did not forget what Tam had done for them. They made sure that Tam and his family never wanted for anything ever again.

(Adapted from a Syrian folktale)

Which is more important for the purpose of atonement: the right words or the right intention? Our story advocates that sincerity of intention is the primary element of atonement. Tam does not know the words of the liturgy. For that reason, others mock him. However, we are taught: "One pure tear in the eye is dearer to God than wine-rituals." So Tam's very special jar of tears is a more pious and precious prayer than the perfunctory recitations of the others in his *minyan*.

Why did the others make fun of Tam? What was the meaning of the jar of tears Tam offered as his prayer? Do you think that what Tam did can be called prayer? Why do you think that God chose Tam? What does this story teach us about atonement?

Repentance for sinners is like medicine for illnesses.

(Judah Alharizi)

Repentance is a key that opens any lock.   (Folklore)

One pure tear in the eye is dearer to God than wine-rituals.

(T. Shapira)

If the gates of prayer are shut, the gates of tears are not.

(Talmud)

· KEDOSHIM ·

Love your neighbor as yourself. Leviticus 19:18

->>> <<<-

The Power of Friendship

SAMUEL BEN NAHMAN lived almost seventeen centuries ago in Palestine. He was a great teacher, a person we call an *amora*. Several times in his life, Samuel left Palestine to go to Babylonia, where most of the great teachers and academies of the time were found. In the course of his visits, he befriended a man named Avlet, a non-Jew who had achieved a well-known reputation for predicting the future by charting the paths of the stars.

Once, during one of his trips, Samuel and Avlet walked down to a pond where they sat down and talked the morning away. Not long after they had arrived, they noticed a group of workers who had come to the pond to cut down the reeds that grew along its edges. Once dried, these reeds could be sold in town to those who used them to make instruments like flutes, or baskets or mats.

One by one, on their way to the pond, the workers passed by the two friends. As one of the workers walked by, Avlet grabbed his head and closed his eyes. He was silent for a moment or two; then, he opened his eyes and said to Samuel: "I have just had a vision in which that man who just passed was killed by a poisonous snake during the day's labor. Mark my words, my friend, that man will die before the day is over."

Samuel had great respect for Avlet's predictions. He wondered and worried about what would happen.

Nissim, the man Avlet had predicted would die before the day's end, walked over to a spot along the pond's edge and began to collect reeds. Like the others, he pulled them out of the moist earth and cleaned them off in the water. Then he placed the reeds he had uprooted on the grass to dry in the sunlight. He and his friends worked hard all morning. Once the sun reached its highest point in the sky, directly overhead, all the workers stopped what they were doing and sat down together in a circle.

So that no one would go hungry, these workers combined all their food and shared it equally. Nissim was given the task of collecting that day's food from each of the workers. He walked around taking whatever each person had to offer. But, when he reached his friend Huna, he noticed that Huna seemed very embarrassed. Because Huna had no food to contribute that day, he felt awkward and ashamed. Nissim felt his friend's pain. When the others were not looking, Nissim slipped some of his own food to Huna, so that Huna would have something to give to the group. Huna gave Nissim a smile that said thank you and put his friend's food in the basket as if it were his own. After Nissim went around to each of the workers, the food was divided equally, and all ate their lunch together.

All afternoon, Samuel and Avlet watched the men do their work. After many hours, the sun began to set and the men knew that the time to quit work for the day had come.

One by one, they passed Samuel and Avlet, each man carrying a sack full of reeds back to town. Avlet could not believe that his prediction did not come true. As Nissim walked by, Avlet jumped up and asked if anything unusual or dangerous had happened to any of the workers during the day.

"Nothing unusual. It was a normal day for us all," replied Nissim, a bit surprised by the question.

"Then would you mind if I looked inside your sack?" asked Avlet. He took the sack in his hands and opened it.

"Samuel, come here and look at this," called Avlet.

When Samuel came over, Avlet opened the sack to show him a snake, slithering about among the reeds. It was most certainly a poisonous snake, placed in the sack without Nissim or anyone else knowing. Quickly, Avlet dropped the sack and Nissim killed the snake with his staff.

"It's amazing that this man did not die," said Avlet to Samuel.

"Maybe it is not quite that amazing, old friend," said Samuel. Turning to a confused and shaken Nissim, Samuel asked if Nissim had done anything different that day from what he would normally do. Nissim thought for a moment and explained that he could think of nothing different except that he had helped his friend Huna with food to contribute to lunch.

"See, Avlet, there is an explanation. This man fulfilled the mitzvah that calls upon each person 'to love your neighbor as yourself.' Because Nissim performed this mitzvah, he was saved from death."

Samuel looked at his friend and said: "You see, your powers of prediction are great indeed; but the power of a deed performed to help another is greater."

(Adapted from the Talmud)

The mitzvah to love another human being as you love yourself is the basis of our social ethic. In our story, Nissim feels the pain of his friend Huna, who cannot contribute food to the workers' communal lunch. He feels Huna's embarrassment as if it were his own.

Our story provides a good basis for a discussion of friendship.

Who are our best friends? What makes them such good friends? Can you think of an example that shows the quality of their friendship? There is an expression: "A person without friends is like a left hand without a right." What does that mean? Do you think that it is true?

· EMOR ·

The Lord spoke to Moses, saying: . . . There are the set times of the Lord, the sacred occasions, which you shall celebrate each at its appointed time. Leviticus 23:1,4

->>> <<<-

Sacred Occasions

THE BOOK OF PROVERBS teaches us: "The mercy of the wicked is cruel." If that is so, then King Resha was the most merciful tyrant of his day. If meanness were pieces of gold, Resha would have been the richest man on earth.

Among the laws Resha decreed was one forbidding the Jews in his kingdom from celebrating any of the Jewish holidays. Imagine, no shofar to blow at Rosh Hashanah. No *dreidlach* to spin and no *chanukiot* to kindle at Chanukah. No seder. No *megillah* reading and no spiels at Purim. No holidays at all.

Resha was not kidding. He placed guards in all of the synagogues in the kingdom to make sure that no Jews came to celebrate the holidays. The doors to the synagogues were nailed shut and large signs were hung warning: "By order of our king, Resha the Great, Jews are forbidden from celebrating any of their holidays, on pain of death."

Well! This law was enacted at the end of the summer. There were no holidays until the beginning of the month of Tishri— Rosh Hashanah. As the month of Elul drew to a close and Tishri loomed closer and closer, the Jews became more and more nervous. Would anyone go to the synagogues, even though it meant death?

Erev Rosh Hashanah arrived, and the Jewish community held its breath. Resha's guards took their stations at the synagogues to enforce the king's decree. Sunset came and there was silence.

Soon the sound of a shofar was heard in every corner of the

102

kingdom. Guards rushed inside the synagogues to see who had dared to disobey the king's command. In each case, there was no one to be found. No one was seen in any of the synagogues. Yet the sound of the shofar was heard throughout the land.

Ten days later, Yom Kippur arrived. Again the Jewish community held its breath. Obviously, someone had been very lucky on Rosh Hashanah. Whoever had blown the shofar had escaped death. It was not likely that such luck could be counted on again.

Sunset came and there was silence all throughout the kingdom. Softly, a familiar sound became clear. It was the chant of *Kol Nidre,* whose haunting melody was intoned once, then twice, and then a third time. Each time it grew louder and more intense. It was bewitching and chilling.

The king's guards rushed into the synagogue to catch the mysterious *chazan.* But there was no one. They searched up and down the aisles. They opened the ark and looked within its depths, defiling its sanctity. They got down on hands and knees to hunt under the chairs. No one. Yet the melody continued.

When Resha heard about this second instance of disobedience, he was enraged and called for his commander of the guards. King Resha demanded to know why his decree went unenforced. Why had no one paid for mocking the authority of the king?

When the commander of the guard explained that despite the searches no one had ever been found, the king threw him in the dungeon and set out to solve the mystery himself.

Soon Sukot had come. Still there was silence in the Jewish community. Even though word of what had happened passed from one household to the next, the Jews stayed home.

Erev Sukot arrived and the king watched the sun set as he stood outside the doors to the synagogue. He had come early to make sure that no one snuck in before the holiday.

Then from inside the synagogue there came the sound of branches waving in the wind—the *lulav.*

King Resha burst through the door and glared at the four walls of the synagogue. He could hear the sound of the willow, palm, and myrtle branches rustling in the air, but there was no one to be seen. In his anger, he turned over all the chairs and study tables. He knocked over the *siddurim* and the volumes of Talmud on the shelves. With no one to blame and no one to punish, he stormed out of the synagogue, feeling frustrated and defeated.

Simchat Torah came and went, as did Chanukah. While no

Jew left home to worship in the synagogue, sounds of celebration continued to come from inside its walls. King Resha had no choice but to rescind his decree. He knew he was beaten by a power far greater than his own.

Years later, it was said that, during the days of the king's decree, a woman named Nisi brought the sounds to the synagogue by simply imagining the holiday celebration in her mind and turning her gaze silently to heaven. At that moment, God fulfilled the mitzvot of the holiday on behalf of Nisi and her prayer.

(*Adapted from* Sefer Hamasiot)

Holiday celebrations are such important times in our lives. They are full of fun and family and wonderful food. Everyone has a favorite holiday. Imagine living in a land where it was forbidden to celebrate that holiday or any other for that matter. King Resha, the tyrant in our story, passed such a law. Yet, he learned in the end that the power of a Jewish holiday was greater than even his power as the king. Other wicked rulers have had to learn the same lesson. In other lands at different times in history, we have been forbidden from celebrating our holidays. Still, we did celebrate them—secretly in our cellars, in our attics, in caves, and even in concentration camps. It seems that we Jews do not give up easily those things that are very important to us.

Which is your favorite holiday? Why? What do you do on that day? Does your family have any special customs for that holiday? Could anyone ever make you give it up? Are there people in the world today who cannot celebrate their favorite Jewish holidays? Who are they? How can we help them?

· BEHAR ·

You shall not make idols for yourselves, or set up for yourselves carved images or pillars, or place figured stones in
your land to worship upon, for I the Lord am your God.

Leviticus 26:1

→》》 《《←

Rabbi Isaac and the Idol

No one has ever seen a jewel like the one Rabbi Isaac owned.
It sparkled like a thousand stars rolled into one. And, when you
held it up to the sun, you could see all the colors of the rainbow
dancing inside. The jewel had been passed down in Rabbi Isaac's
family longer than anyone could remember. Some said that Moses
and the Israelites had actually brought it out of Egypt on the
day of the Exodus.

It is impossible to own a jewel so wonderful and keep it a
secret. So, everyone in the kingdom knew about it. The king
knew about it, too. He had a large, crocodile-shaped idol which
had two jewels for eyes. When one of the jewels fell out and
was lost, the king knew just where he could get another one.

The king sent a messenger to Rabbi Isaac's home. You can
imagine how surprised Rabbi Isaac was to see one of the king's
own guards at his front door.

"Are you Rabbi Isaac?" demanded the guard.

"I am," replied Rabbi Isaac, in a frightened voice.

"The king wants you to bring him your jewel so that he can
replace the one which fell out of the eye of his idol. Hurry up
and get your coat. The king wants your jewel *now!*"

What was Rabbi Isaac to do? How could he give up this very
precious family heirloom so that the king could fix his idol!

Rabbi Isaac climbed into the king's carriage and rode off with the guard. All the way to the king's palace, Rabbi Isaac prayed for a way out of this mess. Finally, he got an idea!

"Excuse me," he called out to the guard. "Do you think you could stop for a moment so I could get out and stretch my legs? It is awfully cramped in here."

"I suppose that a short break can't hurt," said the guard. "But we can't wait too long. The king is expecting us."

"I only need a few moments," replied the rabbi. "I promise to take just a couple of minutes."

So the guard halted the carriage. Rabbi Isaac walked over to the guard.

"You have been sent to bring me and my jewel to the king. I am sure you have heard about how wonderful my jewel is," said the rabbi, "but wouldn't you like to see it?"

And Rabbi Isaac reached into his pocket and took out a velvet pouch. With great care he opened the pouch and removed the jewel to show the guard. He made sure to hold it up against the sunlight so that it would sparkle.

"I have never seen anything like it," gasped the guard.

"Would you like to hold it?" Rabbi Isaac offered.

"Do you think I could?" asked the guard. "Just for a minute. I promise I'll be careful. I won't smudge it. I promise I won't."

Rabbi Isaac placed the jewel in the guard's hand. When the guard held it up to the sun, he could not believe how it sparkled and shone. Just then, Rabbi Isaac pretended to trip, and he fell against the guard, jarring the jewel from his hand. It fell and rolled down the hill into the stream below.

"You clumsy idiot!" cried the guard.

"Oh, no! Oh, no! My jewel! What has happened to my jewel?" screamed Rabbi Isaac, who had planned this all along. He threw himself down on the ground and began crying hysterically.

"I have lost it forever. All my wealth is gone. How could this happen to me?"

"The king will have both our heads for this," moaned the guard.

But, when the king heard what had happened, he did not have them beheaded.

"What terrible luck has befallen the rabbi! I have lost this jewel, but I will find another to take its place. The rabbi will never have a jewel like that again." And he gave orders for the rabbi to be taken home.

When Rabbi Isaac returned home, he found his front door slightly ajar and a strange man sitting at his table. The stranger saw the rabbi's surprise and introduced himself: "I am Elijah the Prophet," he announced. "You lost your precious jewel on purpose rather than seeing it used in an idol. Because you thought only to uphold the injunction against the worship of idols, God will replace your jewel. Next year at this time, your wife will give birth to a son whose brilliance will be greater than that of the jewel. His wisdom will be far more precious than any diamond or ruby, and you will be very proud."

And, one year later, Rabbi Isaac's wife gave birth to a son they called Shlomo. When Shlomo grew up, he became the great teacher known as RASHI, RAbbi SHlomo ben Isaac. And Rabbi Isaac was very proud of him.

(Adapted from folklore)

Our tradition has gone to great lengths to caution against the inclination toward idolatry. It is well known, for instance, that Moses is not mentioned in the *Haggadah*. Why would the great leader of the Exodus from Egypt be excluded from the retelling of that moment in our history? The rabbis did not want to give the impression that Moses brought about the Exodus by himself, thus becoming an object of veneration in the eyes of some. For similar reasons, chasidic tradition teaches that the prohibition against idolatry includes the prohibition against making idols even of the mitzvot themselves. Neither the mitzvah, nor the hero, nor the element of nature is to become an object of veneration. Yet, each may serve as a conduit that leads us to a glimpse of the divinity that pervades our world, and it is that glimpse of divinity that moves us to veneration.

Our story is about idolatry. Could you have devised a different plan to stop the king from taking Rabbi Isaac's jewel? We Jews have always opposed the worship of idols. "You shall not make for yourself a sculptured image," states the Torah. (Exodus 20:4) What is wrong with the worship of idols?

107

· BECHUKOTAI ·

If you follow My laws and faithfully observe My commandments, I will grant your rains in their season . . . you shall eat your fill of bread and dwell securely in your land.

Leviticus 26:3–5

→》》 《《←

The Wise Shepherd

IT WAS ONE THING for our ancestors to receive the Torah at Mount Sinai; it is another thing completely for us to live according to its teachings. So it is fortunate that there have been some people who are good examples of how to live a life of Torah. A husband and wife, named Akiva and Rachel, are two such examples.

The story of Akiva and Rachel took place almost two thousand years ago when Israel was called Judea and was ruled by the Romans. For many years, Akiva was a shepherd in the service of the very wealthy Kalba Sabbu'a of Jerusalem. All day long, Akiva tended sheep. He made sure that wild beasts did not harm them and that none of them ran off and got lost.

Sometimes, when he was in the fields with the sheep, Rachel, Kalba Sabbu'a's daughter, came to sit with him. She was beautiful and there were many men who wanted to marry her. Yet, she would have nothing to do with them. She loved to sit with Akiva. He was not like the other men. He was quiet and he was humble. But he was also very bright and always had something interesting to say about God, about the world, or about life. Rachel would listen to him talk for hours. Especially, she loved the wonderful stories he would tell. One, in particular, was about a fox and a group of fish.

So, again and again, Akiva would turn to Rachel and tell her the story.

Once, a hungry fox decided to catch some fish for his dinner. On his way to the stream, the fox thought of a clever plan to help him catch the fish. When he saw some fish swimming towards him, he called out to them: "My friends, some men have come into the forest, carrying nets to snatch you for their dinner. Jump up here on my back and I will take you to another stream where it is safe." The fish stopped for a moment and thought about the fox's warning. Then one of them answered, saying: "Thank you for your offer, but we cannot come with you." "Why not?" asked the fox. "If you do not come with me, you will be killed." "Maybe that is so," said the fish, "but we are fish and we belong in the water. You are a fox and you eat fish. If we stay here we might be in danger but, if we leave the water to go with you, we shall surely be killed."

So, said Akiva to Rachel: "We Jews are like the fish. Even though the Romans threaten to kill us if we study our Torah, we are Jews and Torah is our way of life. We would surely perish without it. We cannot live without Torah any more than fish can live without water."

When Rachel heard Akiva speak this way, she knew that he would be a great teacher if only he could get the chance to study with the wise rabbis.

"Akiva," she said one day, "if I married you, would you devote your life to the study of Torah?"

"For your love I would do anything," said Akiva. "To study Torah with the sages would be my greatest pleasure."

When Kalba Sabbu'a heard that Rachel and Akiva had decided to be married, he became very angry.

"You could have your pick of the finest men in Jerusalem. Now you tell me that you are to be married to a lowly shepherd. I will not hear of it, and I forbid you to marry Akiva!"

Kalba Sabbu'a threw Rachel out of his house and vowed never to give her any of his wealth. Akiva and Rachel married anyway. Soon after their wedding, Rachel told Akiva it was time for him to go away to the great rabbinic academy of Yochanan ben Zakkai to study with the famous rabbi's disciples.

For twenty-four years, Akiva studied and gained a reputation as a great scholar and teacher. When he returned home, he brought with him many students. In front of them all, Akiva brought forth his wife Rachel and said: "If it were not for the love and patience of my wife Rachel, I could not have become the teacher I am today. If I have earned your respect, then Rachel has earned twice as much. I owe all that I am to her."

For many years, Akiva continued to teach students all about the Torah, and Rachel would sit under a tree, listening to her husband tell all the stories that she had first heard when he was still a shepherd many years ago. The stories were as wonderful as ever, but they were especially sweet now.

(Adapted from the Talmud)

As a wheel's spokes radiate from the hub of the wheel, so all things in our lives radiate from Torah. The Torah portion teaches that prosperity and security come to those who make Torah the foundation of their lives. No wonder, therefore, that study is the primary Jewish value. According to a folk saying: "The one who lacks learning lacks everything." Without learning, one cannot plumb the depths of Torah. In our history there are many examples of great sages and teachers. The following story presents just one, Rabbi Akiva. Akiva's example is both intriguing and important because it shows us that one does not have to be born to great wealth nor to learned parents in order to become a scholar. All it takes is a good mind and a desire to study. Akiva was fortunate enough to have married Rachel, who encouraged him and supported him with love and understanding, making it possible for him to complete his course of study.

Name some of the wisest Jews in history. What was it these people did or said that lead you to think they were so wise? Were these people considered wise by their contemporaries? In your opinion, what is the most important of all Jewish teachings? Which Jewish leader would you like to learn more about than you have already? Why? Did you know that Jewish study is a lifelong project? Can you suggest some ways for adults to continue learning about Judaism? Which of these suggestions do you think you might choose?

· BEMIDBAR ·

On the first day of the second month, in the second year following the exodus from the land of Egypt, the Lord spoke to Moses in the wilderness of Sinai. . . .

Numbers 1:1

>>> <<<

Finding God Wherever We Turn

Y OSE, SON OF PINCHAS, sat aboard the ship that was bringing him home. Although the distance from Tarsus to Jerusalem was not that far, it would take many days for the ship to make that journey. When the winds were good and filled the sails, they traveled as much as thirty or forty miles in a day. When there was no wind and the sails hung limply upon their masts, the slaves had to put the oars in the water and row. Rowing a huge wooden ship with more than one hundred people on board was a painstaking business, which did not move them more than twenty miles a day.

At least there was an interesting group of passengers to look at. There were merchants, who sat and argued with one another about the price of cloves or wool or tea. They would stand face to face and nose to nose, shouting as if they were miles apart, accusing one another of trying to steal their business. Then there were some idolmakers, who were sailing to Judea to sell their wares. They sat all day long, molding their clay and carving their wood into shapes resembling birds with the bodies of horses or crocodiles with human legs.

Yose watched these idolmakers sell their idols to dozens of people on board the ship. It seemed as if they did not have to go to Judea to get rich. All they had to do was ride this ship on its way to Judea and back. They could sell as many idols as they could make. They could earn a fortune without ever leaving the ship!

"Why do people buy those things?" Yose mumbled under his breath. They even tried to sell him one. It was a funny-looking statue with the head of a huge bull and the body of a lion.

"I can't believe it," said Yose. "I saw that guy take a plain lump of clay and mold that statue just yesterday. He used the same clay I find by the river back home, and today he tried to convince me it was a god! It's like the rabbis teach: 'The world is in the hands of fools!' "

Yose had been so involved in his daydreaming that he had not noticed the clouds which had gathered. They were black and their shadows darkened the sea. Rain began falling in torrents. It did not take long for everyone to flee for safety.

For hours, the passengers huddled below deck waiting for the storm to subside. Yet, each hour the rain seemed to fall harder. Little children sobbed out of fear. Adults began to get frightened, too. Most had never seen such a storm. Everyone was worried they would sink right there in the middle of the sea.

Some of the passengers took out the idols they had bought on the trip. They knelt on their hands and knees and prayed to those statues to save them from the storm. They clenched their fists and pleaded for their rescue. Then they waited.

An hour passed, and it was clear that the idols would be no help. What was there left to do? Everyone had prayed to his or her own idols. Everyone, that is, except Yose. He had watched all the others, but he had no idol.

"Yose, our idols have not saved us," cried the passengers. "Please, you must get your idol and pray for our rescue. Maybe your idol is more powerful than ours."

"I have no idol," said Yose. "But my God is more powerful than your idols."

"Well, where is your God?" they asked. "Go get your God so we can be saved!"

"My God is right here beside me. Wherever I go, my God goes with me." Yose closed his eyes and prayed.

Blessed are You, our God, the God of our ancestors, Abraham and Sarah, Isaac and Rebecca, Jacob and Leah and Rachel.

You performed miracles for them. Please hear my prayer and rescue us in the midst of this sea, just as you rescued our ancestors on their way from Egypt.

And Yose waited. The passengers waited.

After a few minutes had passed, one of the passengers spoke up: "What fools we are!" he said. "How could we expect to be rescued by some God you cannot even see or touch? What kind of a God is that?"

At that moment, the rains stopped. The sea grew calm. The clouds parted to allow the sun to shine through.

"Now, who is the fool?" Yose asked. All the passengers threw their idols into the sea. Even the man who had mocked Yose took out his idol and threw it into the waters below. Then he turned and walked over to Yose.

"Do you suppose you could teach me about this God you cannot see but who is with you wherever you go?" he asked.

Yose nodded.

(*Adapted from the Jerusalem Talmud*)

The psalmist has written: "Where can I escape from Your spirit?/ Where can I flee from Your presence?/If I ascend to heaven, You are there;/if I descend to Sheol, You are there too. (Psalms 139:7–8) Even in the midst of the wilderness, God was there with our ancestors. So, we read in our Torah portion: "The Lord spoke to Moses in the wilderness of Sinai. . . ."

In our story, Yose knew that God had accompanied our ancestors in the wilderness. No one carried God. No one could see or touch God. Yet, there were things God did for us that showed God was with us wherever we went. Some people call these special things that God did miracles. What is a miracle? Can you give some examples of miracles? Why didn't Yose believe in idols? Do you think that a statue can have powers like God's? Do you think any person could have powers like God's? If you were Yose and someone had asked you to teach him about God, what would you have taught?

The Lord spoke to Moses: Speak to Aaron and his sons: Thus shall you bless the people of Israel. Say to them:

The Lord bless you and keep you!

The Lord deal kindly and graciously with you!

The Lord bestow His favor upon you and grant you peace!

Thus they shall link My name with the people of Israel, and I will bless them. Numbers 6:22–27

→》》 《《←

Saying Thank You with a Blessing

NATAN REACHED for his water bottle. It was empty. The sun beat down upon his head, making him more thirsty with every step. For three days he had traveled across the hills and valleys of Judea. His home was in Beer-sheba, still two days away by foot.

Since there was no water left, Natan decided to eat one of the juicy oranges he had picked on his way through the Galilee. But when he reached into his leather pouch, he found it was empty too. He must have eaten his last orange many hours ago. Now what would he do?

Until three days ago, Natan had been a proud soldier. He fought with his fellow Jews in their revolt against the mighty armies of Rome. The Jews were courageous even though they were outnumbered by the Romans more than fifty to one. Still, they held the Romans off for several weeks before defeat finally came. Most of his friends had been killed. Others were taken prisoner. He had escaped. Now, with Roman soldiers all over the main roads, Natan had to keep to the ancient back roads and nomadic trails. He had to stay away from the towns and villages. So, unless he found food and water on his own, he had nothing to eat nor drink.

The sun was very hot. Natan's tongue was as dry as a rug. The inside of his mouth had become swollen and the skin on his lips had begun to split.

"Is this it? Have I survived a war in order to die here in the wilderness?"

What could he do? Stop. No, to stop was to die. So he forced himself to put one foot in front of the other and trudge, trudge along.

Up ahead Natan saw a tree. "This cannot be, can it?" he asked himself. "It must be a mirage. It's just my head playing tricks on me," he told himself.

But, as he got closer to the tree, he knew it was not a mirage. It was a tree, a real tree—an apple tree. He started to run. From where he got the energy even he did not know. Now he was running hard; when he got to the tree, he threw himself under its shady branches.

"Ah!" he cried. "Cool shade."

Exhausted, he fell asleep under that tree for hours. By the time he awoke, the sun was beginning to set and the sky was turning purple and orange. He stretched his arms and legs and wiped the sleep from his eyes.

"A few hours sleep and I feel like a new person," he said. As he stood up, he reached above to pick an apple from a branch. Never had any fruit looked so good. He was so hungry and the juicy fruit satisfied his thirst. He gobbled up one apple, then another, and then another.

"Apple tree," said Natan, "you may not know it but you saved my life. What can I do to show my gratitude?"

So, Natan paused to consider what he might do for this tree.

"Can I give you anything?" he wondered. Then he looked down at his torn clothes. "It certainly does not seem that I have anything to give. Well, you can see for yourself that I have nothing but my empty pouch and these soiled clothes. I have nothing to give you."

So he paused to think some more. He sat down with his back

up against the trunk of the tree. He brought his knees up under his chin and wrapped his arms around his legs as he closed his eyes in thought.

"Who says I have nothing to give you!" he cried. He jumped to his feet with real excitement. "Everyone has something to give, no matter how poor he is. A blessing! I can give you a blessing! A blessing is a gift everyone has to give."

But what kind of blessing does one give a tree? Natan knew some blessings. He knew the blessing over the wine and over the bread. He knew the Priestly Blessing that Moses and Aaron had blessed his ancestors with during their days of wandering in the desert. But what kind of blessing could he give to this tree?

He thought for a moment more.

"I cannot bless you with long life, for a great tree such as you has already been here on this earth for many years. I cannot bless you with ripe, juicy fruit, for your branches already have luscious apples growing all over. . . ."

Stumped only for an instant, Natan snapped his fingers and said, "I have it. My blessing for a tree as noble and gracious as you is for all trees planted from your seeds to grow up as wonderful and giving as you." And so Natan blessed the tree and made ready to leave.

A full moon had come out and had cast its moonbeams over the face of the earth, giving Natan a chance to sneak over the old, hidden paths during the night when most of the Roman soldiers would be asleep in their camps. The tree had saved his life and Natan just knew he would make it back to his family in Beer-sheba.

(Adapted from the Talmud)

This blessing is also called *Birkat Kohanim,* the "Priestly Blessing," because originally it was bestowed upon the people by Aaron and his sons and, in later years, by Aaron's priestly descendants. It is one of the oldest blessings we have as a people. Today, you may see rabbis bestow it upon their congregations as a benediction at the end of services, upon a bride and groom at a wedding, upon a baby at a *berit milah/berit banot* ceremony, or upon a bar/

bat mitzvah. Certainly, this blessing, like so many others, is used at very special times. In our story, Natan decides to use a different blessing as a gift to the tree that saved his life.

What does Natan do to thank the tree? Why does he choose that way of saying thank you? When do we say blessings? What do we use blessings for? Do you know the Hebrew words that begin almost all our blessings? Make up a blessing to say thank you for something special in your life by using those Hebrew words and, then, completing the blessing in English.

· BEHA'ALOTECHA ·

When they were in Hazeroth, Miriam and Aaron spoke against Moses because of the Cushite woman he had married: "He married a Cushite woman!"   Numbers 12:1

➤➤➤ ⫷⫷⫷

The Pebbles

Yenta Pesha was a gossip. No secrets were safe around her. There was the time, for instance, when Gittel Hanna decided to go on a diet to lose a few pounds. Well, Yenta Pesha spread the word that Gittel Hanna had to lose fifty pounds to save her marriage. She was so heavy that her husband could no longer tell if he was married to a woman or a cow! Then, who could forget the time that Berel confided that he was putting away an extra coin here and an extra coin there to buy his wife something special for their anniversary. Yenta Pesha spread the rumor that Berel had a fortune saved in his mattress. A group of thieves heard the rumor and split open Berel's bed, looking for this fortune. Since Berel had managed to save only a few coins, however, he kept the money in his cap, under the brim. Although the thieves did not steal his savings, they did frighten ten years of life out of Berel and his wife when they returned home to find the terrible mess. Another time, Yenta Pesha was in the General Store, buying some candles and fabric, when she overheard Yankel bragging about "the new addition to the family which was expected to arrive, with God's help, in just a few days." Well, Yenta Pesha could not believe the news. She ran out of the store, telling everyone she met that Yankel's wife Manya had been blessed with a child in her old age. "Just like Sarah, our matriarch," she said. Yet, the truth was that it was Yankel's cow, and not his wife, that was expecting to give birth!

You can imagine that, when people saw Yenta Pesha coming, they ran the other way. They crossed to the other side of the street. They stopped talking. They changed the topic of conversation. Some of the townsfolk got so angry that they decided to go to the rebbe to ask him to do something about Yenta Pesha.

Into his study they went. Steam seemed to rise from their ears, they were so enraged.

"Rebbe, you must do something about Yenta Pesha. Her gossip is ruining our lives."

So the rebbe sent for Yenta Pesha.

She scurried into the rebbe's office just as fast as her legs could carry her. She was all excited. Flushed and out of breath, she plopped down into the chair opposite the rebbe's desk. She huffed and puffed and picked up some papers off the rebbe's desk in order to fan herself. Rapidly, she waved the crumpled papers in front of her face and created a breeze that almost blew the rest of the rebbe's work off his desk. He had to jump forward and throw himself on the pile to guard it from the force of the hurricane Yenta Pesha had created.

"Rebbe, you sent for me?" Yenta Pesha finally asked. "What can I do for you? There isn't anything wrong, is there? If there was something wrong, you could tell me, Rebbe."

"Yenta Pesha," the rebbe began. "I sent for you to keep peace in this town. You have angered so many people with your gossip that there is no telling what they will do if I cannot stop you."

"Rebbe, so I tell little stories. What harm can little stories do? Why I recently heard one about you. You were coming out of the *shul* last Shabbat and . . ."

"That's quite enough, Yenta Pesha," interrupted the rebbe. "You think that because the stories are little they hurt others less. I want you to go outside and gather a handful of pebbles. Go, go, and quickly gather the pebbles and return to me."

Yenta Pesha looked at the rebbe, wondering if he had been working too hard.

"Go ahead, Yenta Pesha, as quickly as you can," urged the rebbe.

Well, Yenta Pesha had enough respect for the rebbe to do as he wished, even if it seemed very foolish. So she went outside and picked up as many pebbles as she could from around the rebbe's house. When she had a handful, she returned to the rebbe.

The rebbe took the pebbles from her hand and spilled them on his desk. He picked one up and held it in frount of Yenta Pesha.

"This is just a little pebble. Yenta Pesha, please place it back where you found it."

Yenta Pesha was now sure that the rebbe *had* been working too hard. "Rebbe, who remembers where a little pebble like that goes?"

"So," said the rebbe. "This pebble is too small and insignificant for you to take much notice of it or where it came from."

Then, the rebbe flung the pebble toward the window! It shattered the glass and sent shards flying every which way.

The rebbe had Yenta Pesha's attention. He continued.

"It was too small for you to take notice of it, yet it was powerful enough to break the window glass, just as your small stories were powerful enough to break the hearts and trust of your friends. After a while, you may not even remember the source of your stories, but rest assured that they hurt nonetheless."

The rebbe bent over the table and scooped up the remaining pebbles. He placed them in a small bag and gave the bag to Yenta Pesha. From that day on, she wore the bag around her neck. It reminded her of the rebbe's shattered window and the fragile trust that friends share.

A folk saying states: "A tongue can be a dangerous weapon." Certainly, Yenta Pesha's tongue was dangerous. It caused others great pain. The Midrash teaches us: "Even if all of a slander is not believed, half of it is." Even if Yenta Pesha's stories were accepted only partially, it was enough to damage someone's reputation in the community.

Why did Yenta Pesha's gossip hurt others so much? Does gossip always hurt other people? What was the point of the rebbe's lesson? Do you think that Yenta Pesha learned the lesson? Can you think of a different way the rebbe might have taught Yenta Pesha a lesson?

· SHELACH-LECHA ·

The Lord spoke to Moses, saying, "Send men to scout the land of Canaan. . . . "At the end of forty days they returned from scouting the land. They went straight to Moses and Aaron and the whole Israelite community at Kadesh in the wilderness of Paran, and they made their report to them. . . . "We cannot attack that people, for it is stronger than we." . . . The whole community broke into loud cries, and the people wept that night.

Numbers 13:1–2, 25–26, 31; 14:1

→》》 《《←

Rabbi Israel Meets the Enemy

Many years ago, in the village of Horodenka, there lived Israel, the son of Rabbi Eliezer. It was Israel's job to help the schoolmaster of Horodenka by walking the children in the village to school each morning. Then, in the evenings, when school was over, Israel would lead all the children back to their homes.

At dawn, Israel went from house to house, calling to each of the children: "Come along, come along, the study of Torah awaits us all." When the children had gathered in the town square, Israel would turn on his heels and begin the march to the school. On his way, Israel would sing, and soon he taught his song to his little followers: "Yah bah bam, yah bah bam, praised be the Infinite One, Amen." They all sang as they walked. Their voices filled the air so that the people of Horodenka heard the children on their way.

One morning, Israel went to gather the children as usual. Once together, they began to sing, and on that day their voices rose above the little homes of the village, above the trees, and all the way up to the heavens. The angels heard the singing and were very pleased. The song of the children reached all the way into the chamber of the Infinite One, praised be God. Their songs pleased God very much.

Woe to the children, for their song also reached the hearing of Satan, the Evil One. "Listen to that," cried the Evil One to his wicked demons. "Those children must be stopped. They are interfering with my evil plans." So Satan sent one of his demons to put an end to Israel and his song. Once on earth, the demon assumed the shape of a large, fearsome wolf and waited behind an old, thick tree for Israel and the children to pass by.

Soon the demon heard the children coming. There was the voice of Israel leading his followers in song: "Yah bah bam, yah bah bam, praised be the Infinite One, Amen." When the group got close to where the demon was hiding, he jumped out from behind the tree, growling ferociously and showing his large, menacing teeth.

The children were frightened and ran away screaming. When the people of Horodenka heard what had happened, they were very frightened. For days, afterwards, they would not allow their children to go with Israel to school.

"Evil cannot be allowed to prevent the study of Torah," thought Israel. He recalled something his father, Rabbi Eliezer, once told him: "My son, know that the enemy, the Evil One, will try to keep you from Torah and mitzvot. But remember that God is always with you, like a lantern lighting your way. Believe in God's goodness and you will always be safe."

Thinking about his father's words, Israel grew determined. He would go out there and look the enemy right in the eyes. He would show him that he was unafraid.

So Israel returned to where the demon was hiding. As always, he sang as he walked: "Yah bah bam, yah bah bam, praised be the Infinite One, Amen." Once again, the demon in the form of a wolf leaped from behind the tree. He growled fiercely, revealing his sharp, terrifying teeth.

Israel did not flinch. He stood before that gigantic creature and continued to sing. When the demon saw that Israel was not afraid, he grew larger and larger until he was as tall as a house.

Still, Israel did not flinch. He continued to sing and, suddenly, walked straight ahead and climbed up the furry coat of the wolf. The wolf was so surprised by Israel's valiant attack that his mouth hung open, frozen in disbelief. Israel saw the open mouth and climbed inside. There, inside the demon, disguised as a giant wolf, Israel crawled down into the chest of this evil creature. Ahead of him he saw the dark, glowing heart of the demon. Here was his chance. He could pull out the demon's heart. He reached for the beating black heart. And then he stopped. For there in his hands he felt the heart beat, and he recalled his father's teaching: "Pray for your enemy as you would for yourself, for all life is sacred."

At once, he released his hold on the demon's heart and climbed back out his mouth and down the length of his body.

No sooner had he arrived back on the ground when a terrible tremor shook the earth, causing a rumble like thunder. Suddenly, the ground beneath the demon opened and swallowed up the demon. Then the shaking ceased and all was quiet. The Evil One had been defeated.

From that day forward, the children of Horodenka resumed their daily trip with Israel to the school. They always sang as they went, for they knew that their faith in God would protect them.

Israel grew up to become a great teacher, the one we call the Ba'al Shem Tov, the "Master of the Good Name." Rabbi Israel, Ba'al Shem Tov, never forgot his special song, nor did he forget his encounter with the enemy.

(Adapted from chasidic folklore)

Chasidic lore reminds us that, if people carry their own lanterns, they need not fear the darkness. All of us have felt fear. Moments at school, at work, in our homes, in the presence of certain people have engendered anxiety, butterflies in our stomachs. Our mouths run dry, our pulses throb, the blood drains from our head, our hands become clammy. Those who carry their own lanterns, however, are the ones whose inner strength and beliefs enable them to meet their fears head-on and triumph over them. David must have been a bit fearful when he met Goliath, and Deborah a bit apprehensive when she confronted enemy armies. Yet, their faith in God, in themselves, and in their causes burned so intensely that their fears were consumed.

Rabbi Israel met his demon head-on as well. Do you think Rabbi Israel was scared? What gave him the courage to climb inside the demon? Why didn't he destroy the demon when he had the chance? What would you have done? Have you ever shown real courage in a situation? Who are the most courageous Jews in our history? What did they do that was so brave? Do you think they were afraid? What did they believe in that made them brave? Do you share any of the same beliefs held by David, Deborah, Moses, or Rabbi Israel?

· KORAH ·

Now Korah, son of Izhar son of Kohath son of Levi, betook himself, along with Dathan and Abiram sons of Eliab, and On son of Peleth—descendants of Reuben—to rise up against Moses, together with two hundred and fifty Israelites, chieftains of the community, chosen in the assembly, men of repute.   Numbers 16:1–2

-》》 《《-

Who's the Leader Here?

RABBI JOSHUA BEN LEVI was in the middle of a lesson. His students sat on the dirt floor, listening intently to Rabbi Joshua. He spoke softly, and the students had to lean forward with the utmost silence to hear what he had to say. For hours they sat together on the floor. Rabbi Joshua sat with them in the circle they had formed. From time to time, his eyes would close as he spoke. It was at these times that his students thought he was directly in touch with God, getting that part of the lesson straight from heaven.

This day Rabbi Joshua was discussing leadership.

"Once there was a snake. One look at it and you would think it was just an ordinary snake. It was about eight feet long with a head at one end and a tail at the other. Nothing special.

"Nothing special—until you heard it talk. A talking snake is something different. How often have you ever heard a snake speak? But this snake was even more unusual than you might think. Not only did words come out of its mouth, hissing and spitting across that long, forked snake tongue, but words also came out of its tail!

"For years and years, the snake crawled over the face of the earth. It slithered up tree trunks, around large rocks, and through the tall grass. Quietly, without protest, the tail faithfully followed the rest of the body. Until one day it had had enough.

" 'Wait just a minute!' it called. 'I am not budging from this spot.'

" 'What do you mean you're not budging from this spot. Come on, we have places to go. Stop this foolishness and let's go,' replied the head.

"But the tail would not move. This made it very difficult for the head to pull the rest of the body. How far do you think you would get if your tail decided to stay put?

" 'What's the matter?' asked the head, anxious to find out what this was all about.

" 'I'll tell you what's the matter,' snapped the tail. It was quite angry and its tone of voice was harsh. 'For all these years, I have followed you. I have gone wherever you wanted to go. We've gone through muddy marshes and freezing cold streams. We've traveled over hot rocks and across rough wilderness. I am tired of following you all the time. Maybe it's time you followed me for a change.'

" 'Follow you!' exclaimed the head in disbelief. 'Heads don't follow tails. That's not the way it was meant to be. Do you have eyes to lead you? Do you have a tongue which searches the air for the scent of food or danger? Do you have a mouth to swallow dinner?'

" 'None of that matters,' answered the tail. 'All that matters is that I will not budge until you have allowed me to lead for a while.'

"What could the head do? It certainly could not move very easily without the cooperation of the tail. So it gave in to the tail's demand.

"The tail was overjoyed to be in the lead. But trouble surfaced right away. No sooner had the tail begun to lead then it bumbled its way into a sticker bush. Each thorn tore into its hide and left deep cuts.

" 'What are you doing,' cried the head in pain.

" 'Just be quiet and let me lead,' the tail called back.

"Finally out of the sticker bush, they next crawled into the nest of a mother bird and her babies. The last thing the mother bird wanted to see in her nest was a snake. But, without the forked tongue, the tail was not able to smell the scent of these birds and into the nest it went. You can imagine the mother bird's reaction. She flapped her wings in anger and jumped upon the snake, pecking at it with her sharp beak and tearing at it with her claws.

"Somehow, the snake made it out of there alive. But it was sore and bruised.

" 'How much of this suffering do you want to put us through?' moaned the head. 'Isn't this pain enough? Please, please, let me do the leading. You will wind up killing us at this rate.'

" 'No, no. I can do a better job than you did all these years. I just need some time to get used to leading instead of following.'

"So the tail refused to give up the lead. Next, it pulled the head on a journey through the woods. It was night and the snake was hungry. Time to find something to eat. For some time, the tail led the snake through the woods and everything seemed to be alright. Even though it had not yet found anything to eat, it had not fallen into any nests or sticker bushes, and the head counted itself as lucky.

"As it was pulled through the forest, the head thought it detected the odor of something burning, but it could not be sure. After a few more moments, it was sure. There was something burning! Turning around to look ahead, it saw a bonfire blazing just ten feet ahead.

" 'Stop, stop,' it called to the tail, which was proceeding blindly towards the fire. 'There's a fire ahead. Stop or we'll fall into the flames!'

" 'What's this,' called out the tail, 'a new way to trick me. You would say anything to get me to give back the lead. Well, it just won't work. It just won't. . . . Ah!'

"It was too late. The snake had crept into the midst of the fire and had perished there."

Rabbi Joshua opened his eyes and looked out at his students.

"From this we learn: 'As the leader so the generation.' If the leader is blind and witless, the people will be doomed. The Midrash teaches: 'Woe to the community that has an ignoramus for a leader.' "

(Adapted from the Midrash)

This Torah portion deals with Korah's rebellion against Moses and Aaron. Korah incited the congregation and attracted others to his cause, including Dathan, Abiram, and On. Rashi (Rabbi Shlomo ben Isaac), the great eleventh-century commentator, explained that Korah used beguiling oratory to bewitch the people. However, Nachmanides, the thirteenth-century sage, pointed out that Korah's rebellion came immediately after the people had been frightened by the report received from the scouts Moses had sent to explore the land of Israel. Nachmanides says that Korah exploited the fear already planted in the hearts of the people. In either case, it is clear that people have to beware of those who claim leadership over them. It has been said: "The one most fit to high station is not the one who demands it." Our story proves this point. By allowing the tail to assume leadership, the head invited its own destruction.

Did the tail have the qualities needed to be the leader of the snake's body? Why do you think the head agreed to let it lead the way? What lesson did Rabbi Joshua ben Levi teach his students? Make up a moral for this story.

· CHUKAT ·

The community was without water. . . . Moses and Aaron came away from the congregation to the entrance of the Tent of Meeting, and fell on their faces. The Presence of the Lord appeared to them, and the Lord spoke to Moses, saying, "You and your brother Aaron take the rod and assemble the community, and before their very eyes order [speak to] the rock to yield its water. . . . And Moses raised his hand and struck the rock twice with his rod. Out came copious water, and the community and their beasts drank.

Numbers 20:2,6–8,11

Who's the Fool?

DAVID AND LEVI were brothers. All their lives they had lived in the great city. They had never been in the countryside. They had never been beyond the walls of their city.

One day they decided that it was time to venture forth and explore the country. So they set off on foot, through the iron gate of the city and out into the farmland that bordered the great walls.

They walked for a while and came upon a farmer plowing his fields. They watched with eyes wide open in amazement as the farmer guided the large iron plow, pulled by a heavy-muscled horse, in its efforts to dig deep into the fertile earth. As the farmer walked, the ground before him was lifted and overturned so that the mineral-rich earth below might be brought to the surface.

"What a strange thing to do!" cried David as he watched the farmer work. "See how that man destroys the beautiful green countryside. Why would anyone act so destructively? That man is a fool!"

But Levi did not answer. He was curious about the farmer. David wanted no more of this and demanded that they continue on their journey.

"You go on ahead," said Levi. "I want to know more about what this man is doing. I don't understand why he does what he does, but I will believe that he has a reason for plowing the earth and I intend to find out what it is."

So David shrugged his shoulders. He certainly did not understand his brother's interest in this awful man.

As he walked away, Levi heard his brother muttering something under his breath about "my crazy brother" and saw him shaking his head back and forth in disbelief.

After David had been gone several minutes, Levi turned his attention back to the farmer. Levi had to find out why someone would work at a job that seemed so foolish.

The farmer noticed Levi standing there in the middle of his field. He stopped his horse and lowered the plow to the ground. Removing the thick leather harness from around his neck and shoulders, he approached Levi.

"Well, you're either lost or your looking for work," said the farmer. "Which is it?"

"I am not lost, and I am not looking for work," answered Levi. He explained to the farmer how he and David had grown up behind the walls of the city and that this was their first trip ever into the countryside.

"When we came upon you in this field, we could not understand why anyone would ruin land the way you are doing. My brother thought you were so foolish he decided you were not worth talking to and left."

"Come with me," said the farmer. He put his arm around Levi and led him across the field to a hill. Together they climbed up the hill and stopped when they reached the top. From there they could see a whole valley.

"Do you see those rows of wheat and barley over there?" asked the farmer, pointing to a part of the valley filled with golden sheaves of grain.

Levi nodded. "Good," said the farmer. "Last year those rows were plowed just as I am doing to the field you and your brother saw back there. I plow the field to help it breath and to bring all the fertile earth from below the surface to the top. The plow makes long grooves in the earth so that I can plant seeds. Then I wait for the rain and watch the wheat grow."

Levi was just beginning to understand how the farmer uses the plow to plant seeds when he saw something that really upset him.

"What are those men doing over there!" he cried as he pointed to the far side of the valley. "They are taking big swords and cutting down all that beautiful wheat you planted. Quick, aren't you going to stop them?" He tugged at the farmer's shirt sleeve and tried to drag him to where the workers were cutting down the grain.

"Hold on a moment," laughed the farmer. "Those are my own men over there. I told them to cut down that wheat. And those are not swords, they're scythes."

"I don't care if they're swords or scythes," screamed Levi. "Why would you want them to kill all that beautiful, golden wheat?"

"You really have lived your whole life behind the walls of the city. Haven't you ever had bread?" asked the farmer.

"Sure, who hasn't had bread," responded Levi.

"Where do you think bread comes from?" asked the farmer.

"From the bakery. The baker takes this flour and molds it into the shape of a loaf and puts it in the oven," said Levi.

"Where do you think flour comes from?"

"What do you mean, where does flour come from! It . . . ah . . . it . . . well, it comes from somewhere, but I just don't know where that is."

"It comes from my mills. I take all that wheat you see out there and I grind it up with a huge rock until there is nothing but powder. That powder is the flour your baker uses to make bread."

Levi needed to think about this for a moment. First, he found out that plowing does not ruin the earth, it gives the farmer a place to plant his seeds. Then, he discovered that wonderful, golden wheat grows from those seeds. Now, this farmer was telling him that the wheat has to be cut down after it grows so that it can be ground into flour.

"You see," said the farmer, "there are many things we don't

understand right away. You did not understand why I plowed. Now you do. Your brother thought that I was a fool, so he did not bother to understand my purpose."

Levi thanked the farmer for his time and ran off to catch David. When Levi caught David, Levi told his brother that *he* was a fool.

(Adapted from chasidic folklore)

Nachman of Bratslav once said: "Faith is the root and foundation of all holiness." Faith is not blind, as some people may say. Faith is an expression of extreme trust, often derived from much experience. Children raised in a loving and honest family do what their parents tell them to do in a crisis because of the fidelity which exists in their relationship. God told Moses to speak to the rock. Moses struck the rock instead. After all that God had done for him and his brethren, Moses demonstrated a lack of faith which, the rabbis tell us, contributed to God's decision to prohibit him from entering the Promised Land.

Why do you think that Moses struck the rock and did not speak to it as God had told him to do? Why do you think God brought water out of the rock even though Moses had disobeyed God? What would you have done if you were Moses? In our story, why did David call his brother "crazy" for staying to watch the farmer? What lesson did Levi learn at the end of the story? Can you find similarities between Moses in the Torah portion and David in our story?

· BALAK ·

Balak son of Zippor, who was king of Moab at that time, sent messengers to Balaam son of Beor in Pethor, which is by the Euphrates, in the land of his kinsfolk, to invite him, saying, "There is a people that came out of Egypt; it hides the earth from view, and it is settled next to me. Come then, put a curse upon this people for me, since they are too numerous for me; perhaps I can thus defeat them and drive them out of the land.   Numbers 22:4–6

→》》 《《←

Isaac Luria and the King

ONCE, MANY CENTURIES AGO, there lived a man named Isaac Luria. He spent much of his time studying the deepest mysteries of the Jewish tradition and became known for his ability to do wondrous things. Some say that each night his soul would leave his body and ascend through all the heavens to the seventh heaven. There, at the foot of God's throne, Luria would join in study with the greatest of all sages. Just before dawn, his soul would return to his body, and he would spend the day teaching about the secrets he had learned in heaven.

One day, Isaac Luria sat studying by the stream. From far away, he could hear the sound of men's voices. When he looked up, he saw four men approaching. They walked slowly as if burdened by the weight of some great problem.

"Rabbi Luria?" asked one of them. "Are you Rabbi Isaac Luria?"

"You have found me," replied the rabbi softly. "What is it that would bring you so far to find me?"

"Rabbi, you are our last hope. The king in our country hates us Jews. He has commanded that we pay him a thousand bags of gold or he will kill half of us and throw the other half in prison. We have until this Shabbat to raise the money. Rabbi, we have no hope of raising such a fortune. We have heard that you are wise and know the great mysteries of heaven. Only the greatest of God's mysteries can save us now. Please help us!"

Rabbi Luria saw the tears in the eyes of his visitors. He asked the visitors to walk with him to the side of a well that stood next to his hut.

"Pick up the rope that lies next to the well," he told one of them. "Then throw one side into the well and hold the other end."

The visitor did as the rabbi asked.

"Now, all of you take hold of the rope and pull it up from the well."

The visitors could not imagine why all of them had to pull the rope. It was only one piece of rope. How heavy could that be? It was easy enough to lift and toss in. What reason could the rabbi have to ask them all to . . .

Surprise! The visitors were amazed to feel how heavy the rope had gotten. They pulled and they pulled and they pulled. Finally, they had the rope nearly out of the well when they realized that there was something attached to the other end. It was the leg of a huge golden bed. And fast asleep inside the bed was the wicked king.

"Rabbi Luria, what have you done?" cried the visitors. "When the king wakes up and sees what has happened, we are doomed!"

The king did wake up. Before he knew what had happened, Isaac Luria had shoved a bucket with no bottom into his hands.

"What is this?" shouted the king. "And where am I?"

"You are about to drown in the well unless you are able to use this bucket to empty all the water," said Rabbi Luria.

"How can I use a bucket with no bottom to empty the water in this well?" asked the king. "I am doomed."

"Just as you asked the Jews in your kingdom to do what was equally impossible," replied Rabbi Luria. "You doomed them. But I will spare your life under one condition."

"What is that?" pleaded the king. "I will do anything you ask. Just help me get out of here."

"You must sign this document saying that the Jews have paid

the one thousand bags of gold in full." And Rabbi Luria handed the king the document.

The king took one look over the side of his bed to the water down below, and he signed the document.

"Now get me out of here," commanded the king.

"Close your eyes," said Rabbi Luria, "and I will return you to your palace."

The king closed his eyes. Rabbi Luria asked the visitors to lower the rope back down into the well. After they did that, Rabbi Luria asked them to remove the rope from the well. When they started to pull out the rope, they were surprised to find that it was light again. And what do you suppose they found when they got to the end of that rope? Nothing. That's right! The king and his bed were gone, and the rope was completely dry!

When the king woke up in his own bed, he was soaked with sweat.

"What a terrible dream I had," he said as he rubbed his eyes and wiped the perspiration from his brow.

"Quick," he called to one of his servants. "Bring me the document on my desk."

But, when he looked at the document ordering the Jews of his kingdom to pay him one thousand bags of gold, he found that he had already marked it paid in full. His signature and his royal seal were down on the bottom.

The king was so frightened by what had happened that he never persecuted the Jews again. In fact, he became one of Rabbi Luria's students and, for many years, studied the great mysteries of Jewish tradition.

(Adapted from folklore)

The ancients believed that dark forces in the universe could make all sorts of terrifying things happen. Those who could manipulate such forces gained great power and celebrity in their communities. Some were said to be able to summon the forces through the invocation of curses. Bala'am seems to have been such a person. According to the Midrash; "As Israel relies on words of prayer and blessing, so Balak wanted Bala'am to counteract his foes with words of curses." Ultimately, however, Bala'am's magic could not triumph over God's power.

In this Torah portion, Balak, the king of Moab, hires Bala'am to curse the Jews. Other tyrants sought to destory us. The pharaoh of Egypt made us slaves. Then there was the evil king Antiochus about whom we read during Chanukah. Hitler, the ruler of Germany not so long ago, tried to kill all of the Jews in Europe. Why do you think all these rulers wanted to hurt us? What heroes have saved us from their evil plans? Do you think you could ever be a Jewish hero? What kinds of things can you do to be a Jewish hero? Are there any Jews today who need to be saved from destruction? How about the Jews in Russia or Ethiopia? What can you do to be their Jewish hero?

· PINCHAS ·

Moses spoke to the Lord, saying, "Let the Lord . . . appoint someone over the community . . . so that the Lord's community may not be like sheep that have no shepherd." And the Lord answered Moses, "Single out Joshua son of Nun.   Numbers 27:15–18

-»» «-

The Reminder

IN A CERTAIN KINGDOM, long ago, the people followed a strange custom. When a king died, a royal bird was sent out. The bird flew around. And the person on whose head the bird came to rest was named king. That's the way it was done in this kingdom.

One time a very curious thing happened.

In this kingdom there was a slave who made the fine people of court laugh, even though his face was sad. They thought he was so funny that they dressed him in a cap of chicken feathers, and a belt made of lamb's hooves, and gave him a little drum to beat.

One night, the slave dreamed that a small voice whispered to him. He sat up and tried to remember what the voice had said. But all that came to his head was the soft sound—seeeeds.

"Seeds? How strange!" he thought. What could it mean? All the next day, he puzzled over the strange dream. He could not make any sense of it.

That evening, as he was putting on his hat of chicken feathers, he saw that a number of small seeds had stuck to his feet. Quickly he scooped them up and, because he didn't know what to do with them, he put them into the crown of his hat. Then he ran upstairs to make the people laugh.

But the people of the court did not laugh at him that night. They did not feel like laughing, not even at the funny slave. For their king was dead.

The sad-faced slave crept around behind the king's empty chair and fell asleep. He slept sitting up, with his elbows on his knees and his chin in his hands. And he didn't wake up until he heard a curious sound in the air.

Rubbing his eyes, he peered around. He saw a great bird flying through the castle halls.

He opened his eyes wide, for he had never seen a bird like this before. It was so large that the flapping of its wings sent a breeze through the castle rooms.

The bird flew around the room once. It came so close it almost touched the slave. Hastily he pulled out of the way. Then, on his hands and knees behind the king's empty chair, he ventured to look out again.

The bird flew around the room a second time. The slave crawled out a bit to see it better.

The bird flew around the room a third time—and landed on the head of the slave.

"Ouch!" said he, trying to push it off. "Shoo! Get away from me!" But the bird sitting on his cap of chicken feathers had found the seeds. He sat there and pecked at them greedily.

A great cry arose from the people. "The king!" they shouted. "The king!"

Suddenly the slave felt many hands upon him. He was lifted high and placed on the king's throne.

"Long live the king!" the ladies and gentlemen of the court shouted, and they all bowed low before him.

"Me?" stuttered the slave. "But I am only a slave!"

They paid no attention to what he said. For the great bird was sitting calmly on his cap of feathers, like an eagle in its nest.

"O king!" said the minister. "You have been chosen by the Royal Bird. You will rule over our land for the rest of your life. But you must promise one thing."

"What is that?" asked the astonished slave.

"You must never forget that you are king!"

The new king slowly nodded, and all the people clapped. The trumpets blew and everyone shouted.

The king who had been a slave sat up on his high throne, but his face was still sad.

"Build me a hut," he said without a smile. "Build it right outside the palace door."

Puzzled, the minister ordered a small house to be built just outside the great palace door.

The king directed the workmen to make it a simple hut. It was made of rough wood and had no windows. The door was a stout one, however, and on it the king himself placed a huge lock.

The people of the court walked back and forth, looking at it curiously. When the hut was built, the new king entered it. He stayed only a few minutes. When he came out, he locked the door behind him.

Every year this king issued new laws. One year he decreed that every slave should be set free after working six years. Another year he decreed that a slave should be paid for the work he did and that he could buy his freedom from his master with the money he earned. Quietly, one day, the king decreed that, in this certain kingdom, no man had the right to own another. All who lived there were free men; there were no more slaves. And the king's face was no longer sad. More and more, the people saw him smile.

But so gradually did these changes come about that the people of his kingdom hardly noticed.

What they did notice was the king's custom of going into the little hut once every year.

One day the minister asked, "What are you guarding so closely in that little house?"

"Inside are my most treasured possessions," the king said. "See for yourself." He unlocked the door and stepped aside.

In great eagerness the minister went into the tiny hut. He came out again, shaking his head. "But I see only a feather cap, a belt of lamb's hooves, and a drum!"

"That's right," the king said, smiling. "I made a promise to you that I would never forget I was king. But, at the same time, I made a promise to God never to forget I once was a slave."

And, carefully locking the door of the little hut, he went back into his palace.

(Story by Molly Cone, adapted from "A Servant When He Reigns," Folktales of Israel, Dov Noy, ed.; Gene Baharav, trans., Chicago: University of Chicago Press, 1963; Who Knows Ten? *Molly Cone, New York: UAHC, 1965, reprinted by permission)*

This Torah portion is concerned with leadership: Who will succeed Moses as the leader of the Israelites? God identifies Joshua as that person.

What qualities make a good leader? Molly Cone's story, "The Reminder," suggests that good leaders must never forget their roots. In this case, a slave becomes the new king. Yet, he never forgets that he was once a slave.

What do you think made the slave such a good king? What were some of the good things the king did? Did any of these decisions have anything to do with the fact that the king was once a slave? What are the lessons taught by this story?

· MATOT/MAS'EY ·

If a man makes a vow to the Lord or takes an oath imposing
an obligation on himself, he shall not break his pledge.

Numbers 30:3

⇛ ⇚

A Place Called Kushta

ONCE THERE WAS A TOWN called Kushta. The people who lived
there never broke their word, nor did they ever seem to grow
old.

Not many of the inhabitants knew why they never seemed to
grow old. But, since they were happy and always kept their word,
they had never bothered their heads much about it.

One day a king's messenger happened to lose his way and
wandered into this little town. He didn't stay long, but he stayed
long enough. When he returned to his own country, he brought
to the king a most unusual tale.

"In that place, no one ever grows old!" he said to the king.

The king's eyes gleamed. Immediately he summoned his wisest
counselor.

"In Kushta, no one ever grows old," said the king. "Find out
why!"

Now his counselor knew a great many things. For instance,
he knew why apples fell down, and why birds fly high. He knew
why the earth turned, and why the stars blinked. (Though he
didn't know what would keep the king from growing old.)

"But I don't mind trying to find out!" he said, and he traveled
to the town of Kushta.

He walked up and down the streets of Kushta and looked carefully around. All about him he saw ripe golden apricots hanging

141

from the trees. Everywhere he looked he saw people eating them. The women loaded their aprons with them, the children stuffed their mouths, and the men filled their pockets.

"Aha!", he thought. "This must be the reason that no one in Kushta ever grows old."

So he picked a basket full of the ripe fruit. Strapping it carefully to his saddle, he galloped his horse swiftly back to the king.

The king was very pleased when his wise counselor returned with the beautiful apricots. "I will reward you," he said.

But, instead of keeping his promise, he ordered his guards to lock up the counselor. The king certainly didn't intend to let anyone else learn the secret of never growing old.

In his private chamber, the king sat down and began to devour the apricots greedily. He ate and he ate and, when he had eaten all there were in the basket, he went eagerly to his mirror.

But, instead of making him look younger, the apricots seemed only to have made him look older and, suddenly, much greener too! In a rage, he smashed the mirror and ordered the faithful counselor put to death.

It wasn't long before the king sent another counselor to Kushta to find what it was that kept the people from growing old.

Now, the second counselor was even wiser than the first. For instance, he knew why some numbers are round, and why some are square. He knew why clouds made rain, and why ice melted. (Though he didn't know what would keep the king from growing old.)

"But I don't mind trying to find out!" he said, and he traveled to the town of Kushta. When he reached Kushta, he set about to find the answer to the king's question. He walked up and down the streets of the town and looked carefully around.

All about him he saw great barrels catching the rain. Everywhere he looked he saw people drinking the fresh water from the clouds. The women washed their hair in it; the children bathed in it; and the men splashed it on their faces.

"Aha!" he thought. "This must be the reason that no one in Kushta ever grows old." Quickly he filled a barrel with the rainwater and took it back to the king.

The king was very pleased when the rainwater was brought to him. He ordered it poured into his large tiled tub and promised to reward his counselor immediately. But, before taking his rainwater bath, he secretly ordered his guards to lock up the second counselor. Of course, the king intended to keep the secret for himself.

He stepped into the tub. But, alas, when he arose again, he was no younger and only a little bit cleaner.

Shaking with anger, as well as with cold, the king ordered the second counselor put to death.

"I myself will go to the place where no one ever grows old," he decided, and he ordered his carriage. He traveled with great speed, and he carried with him a sack of gold.

Reaching the town of Kushta, he drove straight to the city square. Curious, all the people gathered round.

The king stepped out of the carriage. He peered carefully about him. Sure enough, no matter where he turned, he saw no person who looked old.

Holding his bag of gold high in the air, he shouted, "A handsome reward for anyone who will tell me what I want to know!"

"What do you want to know?" a young man asked. (He might have been an old man for all the king could tell.)

The king smiled. "Tell me," he said softly, "why the people of Kushta never grow old."

The people looked at each other wide-eyed. Not many of them really knew.

But the king thought they did not trust him. He raised his right hand and said, "I am a king, and you can take my word for it. I swear to you I will reward you handsomely if you tell me your secret."

"It's no secret," one said. "This is a town of trust. That is why it is called Kushta. In our language 'Kushta' means truth. As long as we live we always tell the truth." He scratched his head. "I guess that's why we live so long," he said, as though he had not thought about it before.

Everyone nodded. One of them eagerly raised his hands for the bag of gold.

But the secret didn't sound like anything of much value to the king. He pushed the fellow back roughly.

The townsman looked surprised. "The gold!" he said. "You promised to give us a bag of gold!"

But the king was no fool. Why should he give them his gold for nothing? He took his bag of gold and jumped into the carriage. Wildly he whipped his horses home.

But, strangely enough, when the carriage reached the palace

gates, the king who had broken his word in a place called Kushta was dead.

Something even stranger began to happen in Kushta. The people, who had never grown old before, suddenly began to grow older.

When the king broke his promise in the town of truth, the spell (if a spell it was) was broken too. People didn't trust each other so completely any more.

And today, if a traveler should happen to stop at the town called Kushta, he would find it hardly different from any other place.

(Story by Molly Cone, adapted from a talmudic tale, A Rabbinic Anthology, C. G. Montefiore and H. Loewe, World Publishing Co.; Who Knows Ten? Molly Cone, New York: UAHC, 1965, reprinted by permission)

Matot/Mas'ey is a double portion. (See the *Vayakhel/Pekude* chapter for an explanation.)

Molly Cone's story, "A Place Called Kushta," is about a town where "the people . . . never broke their word, nor did they ever seem to grow old." Kushta seems to be exactly what Yitzhak Levi Satanov meant when he said: "Truth lives long and yet does not grow old." If the truth brought the kind of magic that granted eternal life to the inhabitants of Kushta, that spell was broken forever by a king who broke his vow. Not only did the king who broke his vow suffer, but all the people of Kushta, too, were affected by his lie. A lie "is a disease which spreads quickly amongst humanity." So the king's lie infected the whole town.

Why does the king die at the end of the story? What happens to the townspeople of Kushta when the king lies to them? How do you explain what happened to the townspeople? What does this teach us about the power of a lie? When you lie, whom do you hurt? The Talmud contains this warning to liars: "The punishment of a liar is that, even when he speaks the truth, none believe him." What lesson is the Talmud teaching us?

· DEVARIM ·

On the other side of the Jordan, in the land of Moab, Moses
undertook to expound this Teaching [Torah].

Deuteronomy 1:5

→》》 《《←

As Sweet As Honey

THERE IS AN EXPRESSION: "Happy is one whose deeds are greater
than one's learning." Well, Simcha, son of Baruch, was a man
whose good deeds certainly far exceeded his learning. He was a
simple man who had apprenticed as a shoemaker after his schooling
at *cheder* was finished. Some of the other boys showed enough
intellectual promise to be sent to the great yeshivah in Lublin.
Simcha, he would have been the first to admit this himself, barely
got through his years in *cheder*. There was never any thought
that he would continue his studies beyond his thirteenth birthday.
Instead, his father, Baruch, found him a job with Nahum, the
shoemaker. Simcha apprenticed with Nahum for eight years and
then, when Nahum died, he took over Nahum's shop.

Even though Simcha was not the brightest person in the town
of Lutzk, he seemed to be the kindest. He worked hard for all
the community charities. He collected food for the students. He
brought clothes for the orphans. He made sure that the elderly
widows had a place to go for Shabbat. He chopped wood for
the furnace in the *shul*.

Simcha was known as a good and righteous man. Even the
angels in heaven knew of his deeds. One day, the angels were
talking about the Jews down on earth. Some of the angels were
proud of our great scholars like Rabbi Elijah ben Solomon, known
as the Vilna Gaon. Others pointed with great glee to our great

teachers like Israel ben Eliezer, known as the Ba'al Shem Tov. Still others brought up the name of Simcha the Shoemaker.

"Simcha the Shoemaker!" cried one of the angels. "How can you mention the name of Simcha the Shoemaker in the same breath with great ones like the Vilna Gaon and the Ba'al Shem Tov?"

"You know that it says in the Talmud that 'deeds of kindness weigh as much as all the commandments'; I say that Simcha has earned our respect because of his kindness and concern for doing all the good he can," replied another angel.

This led the angels into a heavenly argument. Finally, they all decided that Simcha was indeed special. Since he did not have the rewards of being a great scholar or teacher, the angels decided to give him a special present.

A group of these angels descended to earth and searched around the world to find the sweetest honey from the best bees. They visited all the countries of the world and looked into all the bee-hives. From each of the best hives, they removed the purest honey anyone had ever tasted.

When they had gathered enough honey to fill one jar, they went directly to the little *cheder* in the town of Lutzk. There, under the cover of darkness, they smeared bits of honey on each page of one of the books on the shelf.

The next day, Simcha's son, Matok, came to *cheder* along with the rest of his classmates. When it came time for him to open his book to study, he found a sticky blotch of honey on the top and bottom of every page. The honey was the sweetest he had ever tasted. Each time he turned to a new page, there was honey for him to taste. Each time he got to the bottom of a page, there was honey for him to taste.

Matok loved the honey and he grew to love his books just as much. Over the years, his love of learning became so great that Matok became the brightest, most promising young scholar in Lutzk.

Such was the present the angels gave to Simcha. His son became a great teacher and made Simcha very, very proud. Matok had learned to love his studies on account of the honey rubbed on the pages of his first school books. When he became a teacher, he placed honey on the pages of his youngest students before their first day of school. Eventually, the practice of rubbing honey on children's school books became an accepted and much used custom.

And Simcha—he continued doing good deeds whenever he had the chance.

(*Adapted from folklore*)

———————————————————————————

Moses expounded the Torah to the Israelites as parents would to their children. There were vital lessons to be learned before the Israelites crossed the Jordan River and entered the Promised Land. Ever since, parents have made sure that those vital lessons were preserved in the hearts of their children. It was an education which began very early in the life of the Jewish child. Traditionally, as soon as a child began to speak, parents were to begin teaching Torah verses about Moses and the Torah. Parents took children for walks and pointed out the great scholars who passed by in the street. The first day of school started with a breakfast of delicious treats so that children would associate learning with sweetness from the outset of their education. Similarly, in many communities, there existed a custom of placing honey on the pages of the child's first book. Our story presents one tale that serves to explain just how this custom came about.

Why did the angels seek to reward Simcha? Do you think that he deserved such a reward? What do you think of the reward they gave him? Do you remember your first day in religious school? What made that day so special? Do you have any ideas for ways your temple can make the first day of school very special for its students?

· VA'ETCHANAN ·

You shall love the Lord your God. . . .

Deuteronomy 6:5

⇥⇥⇥ ⇤⇤⇤

Rabbi Moshe Leib and the Horse

MORE THAN TWO HUNDRED AND FIFTY YEARS AGO, there lived a teacher named Moshe Leib. He came from Sassov. Wait! You mean you don't know where Sassov was? Let me jog your memory. Find the Ukraine on a map and then zero in on Lvov. That's not far from Sambor or Tarnopol, down in the southeast on the way to the Czechoslovakian and Rumanian borders. Jews had begun to wander to Sassov almost two centuries before Moshe Leib was born. At its best, Sassov could boast a population of 1,500 Jews. Now, there are none.

But Sassov did give the world Reb Moshe Leib. It was said that, when he was young, he wanted to study with the great Elimelech of Lizensk. So, penniless and without food, he walked all the way from Sassov. It was said that all he ever wanted was to bring joy to those whose lives might be forgotten by others: the poor, the sick, the orphaned, the widows, the oppressed. Moshe Leib did not wait for these people to come to him; he wandered all over the countryside seeking them out. He kept a list of all the poor and lonely, the sick and the widowed, and every morning he would go to all of them just to wish each one a good morning.

He spoke many languages: Polish, Hungarian, Yiddish. This

way he could speak to the people in their own language. It was said that, if you wanted to find Moshe Leib, you would not go to the *shul*. Instead, you would search in the marketplace, the inns, or the countryside because Moshe Leib believed that the whole world was God's *shul*.

Once, Moshe Leib was walking around the marketplace. There he saw a huge crowd, watching a troop of acrobats who were passing through Sassov on their way to a performance in one of the larger towns. While everyone's eyes seemed to be glued to the acrobats who jumped and tumbled and flipped themselves through the air, Moshe Leib took notice of the horses and cattle, standing harnessed to their owners' carts. Having shlepped these carts over the hills and through the countryside to reach the marketplace, these poor creatures were tired and thirsty.

So Moshe Leib left the crowd and the acrobats behind. He walked over to the well and filled several buckets with water. Strapping them to his back, hoisting them on a wooden post, he carried them over to where the tired animals stood. He made sure each animal had water, and he gave each animal a pat and a stroke and a kind word.

One of the spectators watching the acrobats happened to glance away for a moment and noticed Reb Moshe Leib watering the animals. He walked over and handed Moshe Leib a coin: "As long as you are watering my horses," said the man, "you might as well be paid."

Moshe Leib looked at the man as he returned the coin. "You pay me because you think I am doing work for you. It is not your work that I am doing at all. Your horse gives me a chance to demonstrate my love of God. For that, you should not be obliged to me, rather, I am obliged to you."

(Adapted from chasidic folklore)

How does one love God? One cannot hug God, nor hold God's hand, nor send God flowers. Indeed, love of God is demonstrated through the kind of reverence with which one reaches out to all of God's creation: the streams, the trees, the fish, the birds, and the people. The Midrash teaches us: "Even those things that you may hold superfluous in the world—such as fleas, gnats, and flies—even they are part of the created world. God carries out God's purpose through everything, even through a snake, even through a gnat, even through a frog." In our story, Rabbi Moshe Leib exhibits his love of God by bringing water to thirsty horses and cattle.

How many different examples of God's creations can you name? Choose a couple of these examples and show how a person who loves God might relate to each of them. Now show how a person who does not love God might relate to each of them. Does loving God make you treat the world and all its creatures differently? Does it make you treat other people differently? How should people who love God treat themselves?

· EKEV ·

Therefore impress these My words upon your very heart: bind them as a sign on your hand and let them serve as a symbol on your forehead, and teach them to your children.

Deuteronomy 11:18–19

→)) ((←

For the Sake of the Children

WHEN WAS MOSES coming down from that mountain? Some people thought he must have died. How could anyone survive up there for so many days without food or water?

"Aaron, when is your brother Moses coming down from Mount Sinai?" asked Reuven.

"Who will lead us out of this wilderness if he's dead?" asked Devorah.

"Aaron, you must give the orders now. Your brother is not coming down," said Benjamin.

"That's enough! That's enough!" screamed Aaron. "My brother is not dead. Do you hear me? He's not dead! Once God has given him the Torah, he will return to us."

"Yes, but when will that be?" asked Leah. "We cannot wait here in the desert forever."

Just then, a terrible clap of thunder erupted from the mountaintop. It cchocd throughout the valley below and sent a chill through the Israelites awaiting Moses's return.

"What was that?" they screamed.

The thunder rumbled again, and all the Israelities stopped screaming. They were too frightened even to open their mouths.

151

They looked up to the mountain and saw Moses, standing before them on a cliff.

"Moses," the people cried, "you have returned to us. Show us God's Torah. Bring it down here for us to see."

"I have no Torah to show you," declared Moses. "God heard your whining and your complaining. How could God entrust the Torah to you? I must give God something to prove that we are worthy of the honor of receiving God's Teaching."

"Here, Moses. Take my gold earrings and my emerald necklace," called out one woman.

"Yes, Moses. Here is my ring and these silver coins," called out one of the men.

Soon all the Israelites were offering Moses the jewels they had gotten from the Egyptians when they fled Egypt.

Moses took the jewels and disappeared in the heights of Mount Sinai. This time he was not gone for days. He was back very quickly and stood on that cliff with the jewels still in his hands.

"God does not want your jewels," said Moses. "All your gold and silver are not worth God's Torah."

"Then ask if God will give us the Torah because of the deeds of our ancestors, Abraham, Isaac, and Jacob."

Moses returned to the mountaintop. Again, he was very quick to reappear before the Israelites.

"The deeds of our ancestors are not enough," said Moses.

"What shall we do?" cried the people. "What do we have that will convince God to trust us with the Torah?"

Standing up above the crowd, Moses could hear the mumbling of the people, trying to find a solution. He waited a long time.

Finally, one woman approached him and said: "Moses, our most precious possessions are our children. We will promise to teach the Torah to our children. We will raise them to love it and live by it. Ask God if this makes us worthy."

Moses ascended the mountain. Just as before, he returned quickly. The people were anxious. They were nervous. Would God accept this last offer?

"Yes," said Moses. "God has said that for the sake of the children you will receive the Torah. Now you must teach it to them so that it will be inscribed upon their hearts, their minds, and their souls."

Moses placed the Torah in its own special ark. From that day on, the Torah has gone wherever we have gone. It still rests in its own special ark, our Holy Ark.

(Adapted from the Midrash)

"Teach them to your children," instructs our Torah portion. Education, the transmission of Jewish tradition from one generation to the next, is a theme that appears often in the Torah and throughout later Jewish literature. "Teach them to your children" has been a central Jewish precept, which has echoed throughout our communities in every age. Indeed, Jewish tradition teaches that children are our most valuable possession. "The pleasures we get from children are far more precious than gold," states one folk saying. In addition to the pleasure children bring to their parents, children also represent the future of the Jewish people. This is the message of the story.

What would you have offered God for the gift of the Torah? What do you think would happen to the Torah if no one ever learned to read and understand it? Who are the people who have the responsibility to teach children about the Torah? Who teaches you about the Torah? Who are some of the Jewish heroes and heroines we learn about in the Torah? What kinds of things does the Torah teach us about how we should live and what we should do? When you grow up and have children of your own, what will you do to make sure they learn about Torah?

· RE'EH ·

See, this day I set before you blessing and curse: blessing, if you obey the commandments [mitzvot] of the Lord your God which I enjoin upon you this day.

Deuteronomy 11:26–27

⟶⟩⟩⟩ ⟨⟨⟨⟵

How a Fur Coat Tipped the Scales of Heaven

RACHEL DIED. Oh, sure, she tried to fool the Angel of Death when he came for her. She had instructed her family to move her bed to another room so, when the Angel of Death arrived at the house, he would not be able to find her. Then she asked everyone who came to visit her in her sickbed to call her Sarah instead of Rachel. This way, when the Angel of Death came for her, overhearing people talking about some sick woman named Sarah, he would think he was in the wrong house and leave.

The Angel of Death has been around for a long time and has heard it all before. So Rachel did not fool him. Before she knew what had happened, she was floating through a tunnel. Although there was darkness all around her, she felt warm and safe. At the end of the tunnel was a blinding white light. Rachel shielded her eyes as she emerged from the tunnel and floated through a series of soft clouds. Finally she landed.

"Is this heaven? Where am I?" she wanted to know. As she wandered around, Rachel was overcome by the smell of freshly baked chalah. There were *rugelach* scattered all around, along with little candies of all colors, wrapped in clear plastic.

Up ahead, Rachel recognized a group of souls, dressed in white robes, floating through the air. These were on their way to a Torah study session. As they floated by her, Rachel called out "*Shalom Aleichem!*" But no one responded. "Perhaps, they did not hear me," she thought.

Suddenly, from behind, she felt the touch of hands, grabbing at her elbows. She turned around to find two souls, one on each side of her, taking her by the arm as escorts. Together they floated ahead until they approached a huge cloud bank.

They continued straight through it. Rachel thought this cloud was a little damp, and she glanced at her garments to make sure that they had not been dampened by the moisture. To her surprise, they were perfectly dry!

Once they passed through the cloud, Rachel found herself in a huge open space, filled with many other souls. Aside from the souls, there was only one object in the space—a huge scale. It stood with its broad base embedded in a cloud and its pole stretching far upward into the heavens. Two pans hung on either side of the pole, suspended there by chains which attached to a crossbar at the top of the pole. At the moment, the pans hung in perfect balance. All in all, except for its size, it looked like any scale Rachel had ever seen in the marketplace and shops of her old town.

Despite the crowd of souls surrounding her, Rachel found herself standing in complete silence. Suddenly, two souls emerged from behind the cloud. Each carried a huge, bulging bag, placed at either side of the scale.

"Rachel," called out a loud voice. The source of the voice was invisible and Rachel could not tell from where it was coming.

"Rachel," the voice called again. "The time has come to determine where you shall spend eternity. Will it be here among us or will it be somewhere else? We cannot mention the word here but you know what we mean? In the two bags before you are all the deeds you performed in the land of the living. The bag on the left holds your evil deeds. The bag on the right holds your righteous deeds. In a moment, the contents of the bags will be emptied onto the scale. We shall see if your righteous deeds outweigh your evil deeds. If not . . . well . . ."

And the voice trailed off. Rachel was about to be judged. So this was how it was done.

First, the bag of evil deeds was emptied. Among its contents,

Rachel recognized a lie she had told her mother when she was very young. Then there was the time she took extra change from the butcher and did not return it even when she realized he had given her too much money. There also was the time when her own son needed her help, but she was too busy with something else to turn to him.

All these evil deeds weighed down the left side of the scale until it tipped very low to the ground. This frightened Rachel.

Then the bag containing her righteous deeds was emptied onto the other side of the scale. She saw the times she had brought food to the hungry. She saw the time she sat up all night nursing her sick son. She saw the moments of true prayer in the *shul*. All these deeds began to tip the scale so that the side with the evil deeds started to rise.

The scale tipped back and forth, back and forth. First the evil side rose and then it sank. Then the righteous side rose and then it sank. Rachel held her breath as she watched to see where the scales came to rest. Where would she spend the rest of eternity?

Finally, the scales stopped moving. Both sides were in perfect balance. Neither side weighed more than the other.

There was a commotion among the souls that had gathered to watch the proceedings. The scales were in perfect balance! What would happen to Rachel?

After many moments, a new soul floated into the area.

"Wait!" cried the soul. "You forgot something. This fur coat fell from one of the bags on the way over here."

A fur coat? Did that represent a good deed or an evil one? Rachel's fate hung on which side of the scale that coat would be placed. Everything depended on that coat.

"Do you have the tag that tells us what kind of deed this coat represents?" asked one of the souls conducting the proceedings.

"Yes, it is right here attached to the collar," replied the soul that had found the coat.

"What does it say?" There was silence.

"It says that this coat recalls the time many years ago when Rachel was returning from the marketplace. It was winter and a bitter cold day. On the way home, Rachel passed a beggar in the street, who was shivering violently. Though she had no spare change to give him for food, she was upset by his suffering and knew she had to help somehow. So she took off the winter coat she was wearing and gave it to him."

With that, the soul took hold of the coat and walked over to the scales. Down it went on the side of righteous deeds, tipping it in favor of Rachel.

So it is taught! "Happy is one who performs a mitzvah, for one may tip the scales of heaven for oneself and the world."

(Adapted from chasidic folklore)

The Talmud teaches us: "Happy is one who performs a mitzvah, for one may tip the scales of heaven for oneself and the world." This maxim underscores the Jewish conviction that what we do in our daily lives counts. In fact, the mystics believed that the effects of our actions rippled through the spheres of the universe like a stone sending ripples over a pond. Rachel's story shows us the importance of every one of our deeds.

How did a fur coat tip the scales of heaven? What lessons can we learn from this story? What kinds of mitzvot can we perform to change the lives of others? Our Torah portion tells us that we have the choice whether or not to do God's mitzvot. Why do you suppose there are some people who do not perform the mitzvot? Is there anything we can do to change this? What was the last mitzvah you performed? What might the next one be?

· SHOFETIM ·

You shall appoint magistrates [judges] and officials for your tribes, in all the settlements that the Lord your God is giving you, and they shall govern the people with due justice. You shall not judge unfairly: you shall show no partiality; you shall not take bribes, for bribes blind the eyes of the discerning and upset the plea of the just. Justice, justice shall you pursue, that you may thrive and occupy the land that the Lord your God is giving you.

Deuteronomy 16:18–20

The Wisdom of the Young Judge

JOSEPH IBN ALFASI was a spice merchant. He owned a small shop in the center of the market district in Fez, Morocco. In the next shop there was a man who sold olive oil. His name was Meir ibn Kamniel. These two men had operated their shops next door to one another for twenty years. There had always been a friendly competition between them to see who had more customers on any given day. Lately, Meir held the edge because many more people were coming to visit his shop. The spice trade had not been very good in recent weeks, and Joseph could not get his hands on the spices he needed to sell.

After a couple of weeks of watching the customers passing him and walking into Meir's shop next door, Joseph became angry and very jealous. One day, as he was about to close his shop and go home, Joseph noticed a small crack in the wall that separated his store from Meir's. He looked around to make sure that he was alone and then bent down to peek through the crack. There was Meir. Actually, all he could see was Meir's hands and a huge pile of gold coins, scattered on the table. Meir picked up the coins, one by one, and began counting them.

Joseph counted right along with his neighbor. "One, two, three, four, five, . . . ninety-eight, ninety-nine, one hundred." One hundred coins! Joseph was so envious of his neighbor's success that he started to rant and rave.

"Why should I be so cursed? Meir has more money than he needs. Meir has more money than he deserves. I deserve to have that money. It should be mine!" And then he got an idea.

"That money should be mine, and it shall be mine." With that, Joseph ran out into the street, shouting: "I've been robbed! I've been robbed! Please, won't someone help me?"

He ran up and down the street, shouting at the top of his lungs. People came out into the street just to see what all the noise was about.

"I've been robbed!" screamed Joseph.

"Who has robbed you and what has been stolen?" asked some of the curious people who had come outside.

"All the money from today's sales was stolen—exactly one hundred gold coins. It was my neighbor, Meir. I am sure of it. His business has not been very good lately, and he is jealous of my success." And that was how Joseph accused his neighbor, Meir.

When Meir was arrested, he accused Joseph, of course, of trying to take his hard-earned money. The Judge did not know what to do. Neither Meir nor Joseph had proof that the money was his. How was the Judge to make a fair decision when neither man had any proof?

"I need to think about this," said the Judge. "Tomorrow I will make my decision. The court stands adjourned for today."

The Judge left the courthouse and walked out into the city. He walked for hours, here and there. He just walked and thought, with his hands folded behind his back and his eyes on the ground as if he were searching for an answer somewhere in the grass.

Down one street and up another. He turned a corner and found himself in the middle of a school yard. Something the children were doing caught his eye; then something they said made him stop and listen carefully.

Several of the students had decided to play judge. Everyone in Fez had heard about the case of the two merchants, even the children. So one of the bigger students had declared that he was the judge. Two of the others decided to play the lawyers. Two other students played the parts of the merchants, and they stood there before the judge, yelling insults and accusations at each other.

"You are a thief. You stole my money," said one of the students.

"No, you are the thief," accused the other.

Back and forth it went. With all the yelling and screaming, the Judge, who watched silently, thought that he was back in the courthouse at the real trial. Finally, the young student judge said he was ready to give his decision.

"Bring me a bucket of water," he called. And one of the students, who was watching his classmates from the side of the yard, went to get a bucket.

"Put the coins in the water," ordered the young judge. "If the coins belong to the olive oil merchant, the oil from the coins will be seen in the water. If there is no oil, then they must belong to the spice merchant."

"What a wise young man!" thought the Judge. "That's the answer I have been looking for!"

The next day, both merchants stood in the courtroom before the Judge, awaiting the decision. Their eyes opened wide with surprise when the Judge ordered a bucket full of water to be placed before him. He placed the coins in the water just as he had seen the children do the day before. Sure enough, they were full of oil.

"Give the coins back to their rightful owner," said the Judge, "the olive oil merchant." The coins were given back to Meir, and Joseph was taken from the courtroom and placed in jail for the theft of Meir's money.

All the spectators in the courtroom whispered about the wisdom of the Judge. But the Judge knew who was the truly wise one. He called for silence in the courtroom and motioned to someone standing by the door. There stood a little boy, very nervous in front of all those grown-ups.

"Here is your wise judge!" announced the Judge. "He has taught me that wisdom is not always determined by age, nor justice by the person with a title."

That little boy, whose name was Tammim, himself grew up to become a judge. As he grew, so did his wisdom.

(Adapted from folklore)

One of the very first things God instructed the Israelites to do when they reached the Promised Land was to appoint judges and magistrates. Without justice there could be no society. In fact, the rabbis taught that justice along with truth and peace sustained the entire world. Yet, what kind of person would make a good judge? Maimonides believed that "a judge must have these seven virtues: wisdom, humility, fear of God, disdain of profit, love of truth, love for other people, and a good name."

What kinds of qualities do you think a good judge must have? Was the Judge in this story wise to have listened to the young judge? Do you think the young judge had the right answer? Can you think of another way to figure out who was the thief? What kind of a judge do you think you might make? What do you think justice is?

· KI TETZE ·

You shall not subvert the rights of the stranger or the father-less. . . . Remember that you were a slave in Egypt. . . . When you reap the harvest in your field and overlook a sheaf in the field, do not turn back to get it; it shall go to the stranger, the fatherless, and the widow. . . . Always remember that you were a slave in the land of Egypt; there-fore do I enjoin you to observe this commandment.

Deuteronomy 17–19, 22

Standing in the Shoes of Others

ASHER WAS THE WEALTHIEST MAN IN TOWN, but he had not always been so. Some years before, Asher had found a sack with some leather strips, some string, and some buttons inside. The buttons turned out to be gold, and Asher turned out to be rich, very rich indeed.

Asher was wealthy, but he was also stingy. A more miserly individual never existed anywhere. It was said that Asher made his wife sign a contract every time he gave her money for food or for clothes. It was said that he collected the crumbs left over from a meal and ordered that they be used again in the next day's meal. It was said that, when he wore holes in his shoes, he did not throw them away; he had all the good leather saved and made into shoes for his children.

Everyone in town knew of Asher's reputation for stinginess. So, when it came time for the rabbi to ask Asher to help a family that had no money to buy wine and candles and food for the upcoming holidays, the rabbi knew he had to have a very clever plan.

The rabbi waited to visit Asher on a bitterly cold day. The wind was howling and snow was blowing everywhere. Even the cats and dogs that usually roamed the streets found some shelter. No one ventured outside; rather, this day was one for extra wood in the furnace and someone to cuddle with to keep warm.

Therefore, it was a surprise for Asher to hear the bang of the large iron door-knocker. At first, he thought that it had to be the wind assaulting the door. Then, when it persisted, he left his seat in front of the fireplace in his study, wrapped himself in a blanket, and trudged to the door. Getting up from the warmth of the fire put him in a more surly mood than usual. By the time he reached the door he was really angry.

"Rabbi, what are you doing here?" Asher snapped as he opened the door.

"Well, well," said the rabbi, "and a good morning to you, too."

"I suppose you might as well step inside," said Asher. His invitation was not very cordial.

"Well, well," said the rabbi as if he had not even heard Asher's invitation to come in out of the cold. Yet, he had heard Asher.

"Please, Rabbi," Asher insisted, "come inside. The wind is howling and we would be more comfortable inside."

"Reb Asher," continued the rabbi as if, again, he had not heard a word that Asher had said. "You know the holidays are coming. Our community will be preparing to celebrate and . . ."

Asher was growing impatient. "The cold must have made the rabbi deaf," he thought. So he shouted, "Rabbi, let's go inside and have some brandy by the fire. Then we can discuss whatever you wish."

But the rabbi just continued as if Asher had never opened his mouth. "Soon, everyone will be out shopping at the market. There is so much to get ready. Still, the time is so festive. It is a wonderful time, don't you think, Reb Asher?"

"Yes, Rabbi, a wonderful time." He grabbed for the rabbi's arm in order to lead him inside.

"Reb Asher, do you remember the days when you were poor?

Do you remember how you felt when the holidays came and you sought to prepare for them?"

Asher grabbed again for the rabbi's coat, but each time he did the rabbi would take a step further back onto the porch, drawing Asher further and further outside into the bitter cold.

"Rabbi, please, let us continue this discussion in the house!" Asher was shouting now. His face was growing red with rage even as his body was growing blue with cold.

"Asher," asked the rabbi as softly as he could, "why are you so angry?"

"Rabbi, it is freezing out here and you refuse to accept my repeated invitations to continue our discussion inside."

"How long have we been standing here?" asked the rabbi.

"Too long!" cired Asher.

"But it has only been a few moments, hasn't it?" asked the rabbi again. "Once, many years ago, you spent a great deal of time in the cold. You used to go from home to home, asking for money so your family could have food for the holidays. Sometimes you even came to me seeking help. Yet, every time I have come to you for help, now that you are wealthy, you refuse me. Can it be that the warmth of your wealth has helped you forget the bitter desperation of your former suffering?"

The snow and the wind had combined to create an icy frosting to Asher's beard. He shivered and began to recall all those awful days when he would go begging in weather very much like this.

"Yes, Rabbi," said Asher very meekly. "Until this moment, I had forgotten what it felt like to suffer. You have reminded me. What can I do to help?"

It is said that, from that day on, Asher became a real *tzadik,* a very righteous person. Wealth and success can make the memory very short. It's harder to remember the bad times, but every *tzadik* does. That's what it takes to be a *tzadik.*

(Adapted from folklore)

We Jews are a people of memory. It is not only that remembering connects us to people and events long past, but it is, as well, that remembering humbles us. We were not born with all the skills, talents, and friends or loved ones we have now. Memories of times when we "had not" enable us to better empathize with those who currently "have not." Folk wisdom teaches us: "A miserly rich man is worse than a pauper." That is even more true when the rich man was once a pauper. In our story, we encounter such a character. Asher has forgotten what it was like to be poor, cold, and hungry. The rabbi devises a clever scheme to remind him.

Why do you think Asher forgot what his life was like when he was poor? What was the lesson the rabbi had in mind when he went to visit Asher? How does this lesson relate to the verses from Deuteronomy (17–19, 22)? Nachman of Bratslav once said: "If we do not help a person in trouble, it is as if we caused the trouble." Does this saying have anything to do with the story?

Set aside in full the tenth part of your yield—in the third
year, the year of the tithe—and give [author's change in
the translation] it to the Levite, the stranger, the fatherless,
and the widow. . . .   Deuteronomy 26:12

>>> <<<

A Charitable Woman

AT ONE TIME things had gone very well for Rachel. She was
truly blessed. Her life was filled with the needs of her husband
and her children. Let us not forget her farm. It was the largest,
most prosperous farm in the whole Jezreel Valley, stretching from
the river Kishon out as far as the eye could see. Deborah, the
great judge, had led the Israelites to victory over the Canaanites
only a few miles from the farmhouse. Gideon triumphed over
the Midianites just a few miles further to the east. For centuries,
Rachel's family had farmed this land, and when Rachel married
Amos it became theirs to farm together.

It did not take much cleverness to be successful farming this
land. Just about all one needed to do was pick up a seed and
throw it out anywhere. It would grow wherever it landed. So
Rachel and Amos became very wealthy. It took twenty carts
just to bring their vegetables and fruits to market.

When they got to the marketplace, Amos would take seventeen
carts to the merchants who would buy the harvest. Rachel took
the other three carts and paid a visit to the academy of Eliezer
ben Hyrcanus.

"Rachel, it is good to see you again," said Eliezer. "It does
not seem possible that another year has come and gone so quickly,
but here you are. What do you have for the poor and the orphaned
this year?"

"Rabbi Eliezer, it is good to see you, too. This year Amos

and I have brought twenty carts filled with our harvest to the market. We have set aside three of them for those who are hungry," said Rachel as she led Eliezer outside to see the beautiful fruits and vegetables.

"Twenty carts!" cried Eliezer. "You have most certainly been blessed with the best farmland in the Jezreel. But, Rachel, the law requires that you donate only two of your carts. That is the one-tenth tithe. You have brought more than the law asks."

"Amos and I know what the law requires, but we also know what our hearts demand from us."

Year after year, Amos and Rachel brought a greater tithe than the Torah commanded. Their generosity was known far and wide. Then tragedy struck.

Amos was killed in the war against Rome. Rachel had to care for her children, Simeon and Leah, all by herself. Since they were still very young, she had to tend to the farm by herself as well. And she did. And each year she brought her harvest to the marketplace, along with her tithe, which always was more than it had to be.

Then came the pestilence and acre upon acre of Rachel's farmland became infertile. No matter how hard she tried, nothing would grow in her fields. Only one small parcel of land remained good. It was very small and barely provided enough food for Rachel and her family. When she went to the marketplace, she only needed one cart for her harvest. Yet, even though she had so little, Rachel still made sure she had something to give Rabbi Eliezer. Her gift was still more than the one-tenth tithe.

One day, in the fifth year of the pestilence, Rachel was out in the fields with Simeon and Leah. Both her children had grown tall and strong. It was a good thing, too, for it took all their help to grow enough food to keep them all alive. The sun was about to set and Rachel began to collect her basket and tools to go home.

One step, two steps, and thud. Rachel tripped and spilled everything in her basket. Slowly she picked herself up and dusted off the dirt.

"I guess my eyesight is not as good as it was when I was younger," she mumbled to herself. Full of curiosity, she walked back a couple of steps to see what had caused her to fall. Expecting to find a rock or a hoe, she was very surprised to discover a bucket, half-buried in the ground.

"That's very strange," she thought. "What is that bucket doing there, all covered up by dirt? Who could have left it here and forgotten all about it?"

She bent down to uncover it and started digging away the soil. No sooner had she begun when she discovered that the bucket was filled with coins—not just any coins but gold coins.

With her treasure, Rachel was able to buy plenty of food for her family, her horses and donkeys, her cows and chickens. She also made sure to buy extra food to bring to Rabbi Eliezer for the poor and the orphaned. As long as the pestilence lasted, she and her family had food. Just as her last coins were spent, the pestilence disappeared and all sorts of vegetables and fruits grew in her land, even better than they had before.

Each year when Rachel, Simeon, and Leah went to market, they brought with them carts and carts filled with food. As always, they made sure that they kept some of the harvest set aside to give to Rabbi Eliezer. Their tithe was always more than it had to be.

(Adapted from folklore)

The Torah portion does not ask only those with great wealth to set aside the tenth part of their yield. The tithe was the obligation of all, despite one's station in life. No wonder the Talmud instructs us: "Even a poor person living on *tzedakah* should give *tzedakah*." Reaching out to others by giving something of oneself has always been a cornerstone of our Jewish world. Rashi wrote: "Because of acts of love and kindness the world continues to exist."

Rachel and Amos gave more than their share when times were good. Rachel continued to do the same even when times were desperate. Why do you think Rachel continued to give more than she had to give even when she was very poor? Have you ever heard that "whoever gives money to the poor is blessed sixfold; whoever does it with a kind word is blessed sevenfold"? What do you think that means? Does it have anything to do with the meaning of the story? Have you ever thought of setting aside some part of your weekly allowance for those who need help? How can one help other people without using money?

I call heaven and earth to witness against you this day: I
have put before you life and death, blessing and curse.
Choose life. . . .   Deuteronomy 30:19

—>>> <<<—

The Rabbi and the Dove

Rabbi Baki was the wisest teacher in all Lithuania. There was
no question he could not answer. There was no subject about
which he could not teach. Students came from far and wide to
sit at his feet and listen to him teach about the early rabbis called
the *Tannaim* and the *Amoraim* or about the great sage of the Middle
Ages Moses Maimonides.

All Rabbi Baki's students adored him. All, that is, except one.
His name was Tipesh. When he had first heard of Baki's reputation,
Tipesh left his village and traveled to the town where Rabbi Baki
lived. He planned to enter the rabbi's class to ask him a question
the rabbi could not possibly answer. Tipesh, of course, would
know the answer, and thus he would become famous as a wiser
person than Rabbi Baki.

Tipesh successfully entered Rabbi Baki's class as he had planned.
He was silent for the first few classes. Then he asked the rabbi:
"Who, with one blow, annihilated one-quarter of all the people
in the world?"

There was a hush in the classroom as the students awaited the
rabbi's response. Baki knew the answer. "When Cain murdered
Abel, he destroyed one-quarter of the world's population," replied
Baki in a very quiet, soft tone.

Tipesh was enraged. He grew even more determined to find
a question the rabbi could not answer. So the next day he spoke
up again.

169

"Rabbi," he began, "it is written that Noah gathered all the creatures of the earth with him in the ark. Yet, there was one creature that did not come aboard. Which was that?"

Again there was silence in the class. None of the other students could think of an answer. Each searched his memory to recall that section of the Torah. Rabbi Baki remained silent. His dark brown eyes were fixed upon Tipesh. Underneath his long black beard his lips curled into a smile.

"Once again, you have challenged me," he said to Tipesh. "I am grateful for these opportunities to test my mind. In this case, the only creatures that were not aboard the ark during the Flood had to be the fish that swam alongside it all the forty days and nights."

Tipesh flushed with anger. The rabbi had foiled his plan again. There must be a question the rabbi cannot answer. For two days, Tipesh stayed away from class, straining to invent a question without an answer. Then, finally, he came upon a solution.

The next day, Tipesh returned to class. Rabbi Baki welcomed him, as did all his classmates.

"It is good to be back," said Tipesh. "I have been absent for two days because I was troubled by a puzzle. All day and night I pondered this puzzle until I decided that only one person is wise enough to supply the answer. Rabbi Baki, that wise one is you."

"As we have learned from our great teacher Solomon Ibn Gabirol," said Baki, " 'A person is wise only while searching for wisdom; when he thinks he has found it, he is a fool.' So I know that I am still searching for wisdom and have not yet become wise. Perhaps, we can find a solution to your puzzle together. Please, let me hear it."

Tipesh took a breath and then reached into a bag he had brought. With his two hands hidden behind his back, he approached the rabbi.

"Rabbi, I am holding a dove in my hands. Can you tell me if it is alive or dead?" Tipesh had devised a wicked scheme. If Rabbi Baki replied that the bird was dead, Tipesh would simply open his hands to show everyone a live dove. If the rabbi said the bird was alive, then Tipesh would close his hands around the dove and smother it, showing everyone a dead bird. "There is no way the rabbi could solve this puzzle," thought Tipesh.

"How can the rabbi solve this?" whispered the other students. They held their breath as they awaited his response.

Baki closed his eyes and stroked his long beard. Although only a few moments passed, it seemed like forever before he opened his eyes and spoke.

"Tipesh, you have presented us with a very difficult puzzle indeed. In your hands you are holding a life. Choose well what you will do with it. The answer to this puzzle, Tipesh, lies in your hands, not mine."

(Adapted from folklore)

The verse from the Torah portion is about choices, the consequence of the free will with which we are all endowed. We have the power to make the choices which will bring us blessing or curse, life or death. Thus Bahya said: "Days are scrolls, you may write on them what you wish." Rabbi Baki, the wise teacher in the story, teaches one of his students this same lesson. He tells his student that he is holding a life in his hands, and he must choose well what he will do with it.

We each hold our lives in our own hands. What choices will we make? What kinds of choices do you make each day? Are some of these choices harder than others to make? Which are the hardest? Why is it sometimes hard to make the right choice? What helps you to make the right choice especially when it is a hard one to make? What do you think Rabbi Baki meant by his answer to Tipesh?

· VAYELECH ·

Moses wrote down this Teaching and gave it to the priests.
. . . And Moses instructed them as follows: . . . Gather
the people—men, women, children, and the strangers in
your communities—that they may hear and so learn to revere
the Lord your God and to observe faithfully every word
of this Teaching. Their children, too, who have not had
the experience, shall hear and learn to revere the Lord your
God. . . .   Deuteronomy 31:9–10, 12–13

⤏⤏⤏ ⬿⬿⬿

At Sinai

Reuben lay on his back before the tent and blinked up at the
hot blue sky. Throwing one leg over the knee of the other, he
moved his sandaled foot up and down. Slowly he turned his
head and looked at Mount Sinai. Its peak was hidden in soft
gray clouds. Somewhere among those clouds was Moses, gone
many days now. Reuben sat up, his face troubled.

"Reuben," his mother's voice came from the tent, "it is too
hot to lie out there."

Reuben got to his feet. His short tunic clung damply to his
body. He did not take his eyes from the mountain that squatted
in the hot sands. Sometimes he kept watching it all day and late
into the night, when it was swallowed by the heavy darkness.

"Still worried about Moses?"

He turned. His mother had come to the door of the tent, an
earthen jug in her hand.

"Yes," said Reuben, "he has been up on the mountain many
days alone. Do you think. . ."

"Tomorrow," said his mother, "he will return. It is forty days that he is gone." She held out the jug to him. "Run to the well and get some water."

Reuben trotted off, the jug on his shoulder. He made his way in and out between the scraggly rows of tents. Groups of men stood about, talking of Moses. Reuben knew they were restless for Moses' return. He knew by the way they kept turning and looking at Sinai.

The well was behind a cluster of trees at the very edge of the encampment. Jacob and Naphtali were sitting there, scraping pictures in the sand with sharp sticks. They looked up as Reuben came up to them.

"Tell us, Reuben," Jacob grinned at him, "how many days is it that Moses has been gone?"

Reuben said nothing. He lowered the jug into the well and drew it up again, filled with cool, sparkling water. Jacob nudged Naphtali with his foot. "He can think of nothing else since Moses went up on Sinai."

Naphtali turned his suntanned face to Reuben.

"Have you ever seen Moses?" he asked.

"N-no," said Reuben. He shifted the brimming jug to his shoulder. "I have never really seen him. Only from the distance. I saw his head, and when I came closer he was gone."

"I was in his tent once," Jacob said proudly. "It was three days before he went up on Sinai for the commandments."

"What is he like?" asked Reuben eagerly.

"He has a white beard," said Jacob, "and he seemed tired."

"And . . ." Reuben prompted him.

Jacob shrugged his shoulders.

"It is hard to describe him," he said. "Perhaps you will see him when he comes down from Sinai."

"I am going to get up early," said Naphtali, stretching his long arms over his head. "I'll be one of the first to get there. Then I'll be sure to see him."

Reuben turned to go. Everyone would be at Sinai when Moses returned, and perhaps he would not see him then either.

Reuben could not sleep that night. The camp had buzzed all evening with talk about Moses, about the commandments he would bring. No one really knew what they would be, but Caleb thought there would be one about God, and another about the Sabbath. Everyone had tried to guess, talking eagerly near the campfires. At last the fires died down, and the people had gone into their tents to sleep. But Reuben could not sleep.

For a long time he tossed and turned restlessly on his mat. Then he rose, listened for a moment to the deep, quiet breathing of his father and mother, and crept out of doors. A bright moon hung over the silent tents, and from the distance he heard the braying of a donkey. Tonight Mount Sinai was clear under the moonlit sky. Somewhere on the lonely mountain Moses sat. Reuben began to walk toward Sinai. The sand was still hot under his feet, though the sun had gone down many hours before.

When Reuben reached the end of the encampment, he stopped. It was still a great distance to Sinai, and there were no guards posted beyond the tents. Dan had told him only yesterday that he had seen a mountain lion.

Reuben fingered the sharp knife in his belt, swallowed hard, and walked on. His feet moved noiselessly over the ground. This time he would see Moses. He turned quickly as he heard the patter of feet behind him. Joshua, one of the guards, came up to him and peered into his face.

"Where are you going, lad?" Joshua asked him curiously.

"To Sinai."

"But Moses will not return till morning. Then we will all go."

"If I wait till morning I may not see him," Reuben explained eagerly. "There will be too many."

The guard looked at him. He seemed to hesitate.

"Do not go too near to the mountain," he said at last.

And he turned and walked back to the encampment while Reuben continued on his way. He would see Moses. He would be the first one. A cloud moved over the moon. Perhaps the guard was right. Perhaps he should have waited till morning. Reuben jumped, then stood frozen to the ground. A shadow fell along the ground before him. He shifted his eyes from side to side. The shape of a rock loomed up on his left, its shadow slanting toward Sinai. Reuben sighed with relief and hurried on.

The moon sailed out from under the cloud and hung over Mount Sinai. Reuben stopped and looked up. The pearly gray clouds over the peak of Sinai had become black and heavy, and a strange rumbling sound seemed to shake the mountain from its core.

"Moses," whispered Reuben, "come quickly. I am afraid here in the dark. . . . And I have never seen your face."

A gust of wind swept down from the mountainside. Reuben drew his tunic closer about him, clutched his knife in his hand, and stretched out on the sand. The mountain rumbled. Then all was quiet.

Reuben felt a stab of light in his eyes. He opened them and looked about. The bright morning sunlight was streaming over the mountain. He sat up with a start, then scrambled to his feet.

The next moment he saw him.

Moses stood alone on the mountainside, and it seemed that his face was made of light and the light reached up and streamed out in two beams from his silver hair. He stood motionless, a tall figure dressed in white, looking out over the sleeping encampment. Far above his head the shrouded mountain rumbled and roared. But Moses did not stir. The two tablets of the Law in his hand, he stood waiting.

"Moses," whispered Reuben. He took a step toward the lonely figure whose face he could hardly see for the light upon it. "Moses, you have come."

Then Moses turned and saw the boy. Slowly he began to descend the mountain. Reuben stood rooted to the spot, unable to move. It was toward him that Moses was coming. He waited, his heart beating. Then he felt Moses' hand upon his shoulder.

"What is your name, lad?" he heard Moses ask.

"Reuben," the boy stammered.

"I am glad it was you I saw first from the mountain," Moses spoke again, "the young and eager, who waited for my return. It is for those who are anxious to learn that I remained for forty days on Sinai. For you, Reuben. . . ."

The sharp blast of a trumpet was heard from the mountain, so loud that it shook the ground beneath their feet. But Reuben was not afraid.

Standing there beside Moses and watching the people hurrying toward them from the encampment, Reuben's heart sang. For Moses' hand was upon his shoulder and his voice rang in his ears.

(*Story by Deborah Pessin, reprinted by permission of The Board of Jewish Education of Greater New York*)

According to the text (31:2), Moses announces to the people that he is 120 years old. Ever since, it has become a custom to wish someone you love: "May you live to be 120!" With Moses' life near its end, he takes steps to assure the continuity of his people: First, he appoints Joshua as his successor; then he gathers the people and instructs them to observe God's mitzvot and involve their children in that experience. His appointment of Joshua accounted for the Israelites' immediate need for leadership. His call for involving children "who have not had the experience" addresses the issue of future survival. Thus, it is a lesson we should heed today. Involving our children in the ongoing experience of our tradition helps assure the future of Judaism and the Jewish people. In our story, Reuben has an unforgettable encounter with Moses. While our children cannot hope to meet Moses, they can have unforgettable encounters with our heritage and with the leaders of our people.

What do you think Moses might have looked like? Would you have done what Reuben did? Why do you think the mountain rumbled while Moses was upon it? Why was it so important to Reuben to be the first to see Moses come down from the mountain? Why did Moses ascend Mount Sinai? What were some of the commandments Moses brought down from the mountain?

· HA'AZINU ·

⇶ ⬿

Just Like Papa Did

THE POGROMS WERE HORRIFYING. Unfortunately, the town of Grodno had suffered through many of these attacks. The Polish government sent soldiers called Cossacks to raid the town, breaking windows, setting fire to homes and stores, and assaulting anyone who happened to be on the streets. Old women and children were beaten alike. The Cossacks did not care who was hurt as long as they were Jews.

Pinchas heard the thunder of the Cossack's galloping horses as they rode into Grodno. Quickly he swept away the straw covering the dirt floors and pulled open the door to the secret cellar.

"Hurry, hurry Malka," he said to his pregnant wife as he helped her down the wooden ladder, making sure to close the door behind him. He had attached a piece of rug to the other side of the secret door to cover it and keep it hidden.

"Pinchas, they will find us this time. What will they do to us when they find us?" cried Malka.

"Sshh! Quiet!" whispered Pinchas. "They will not find us. Be still, Malka. They will not find us!" And Pinchas closed his eyes and held his hands up to heaven.

"*Ribono shel olam,* Ruler of the universe, hear my prayer." And Pinchas prayed.

The Cossacks did not come to the home of Pinchas and Malka

177

that night. But a visitor did arrive. Malka gave birth to a baby girl that very night, right there in the cellar, in the midst of the pogrom.

"Let's call her Esther," Pinchas suggested. "Perhaps she will grow up to be a savior of her people just as Esther was in the days of the tyrant Ahashuerus."

So Esther was born. On the following Shabbat, Pinchas was given the honor of an *aliyah* in Grodno's one and only *shtibl*. The rabbi announced Esther's birth and said a prayer for her called a *"Mi Sheberach."* After services, Pinchas and Esther hosted a special party in their home to introduce Esther to the community. There were little pastries, filled with nuts and cinnamon, called *rugelach*. There was strong liquor called *schnapps*. The men drank this in little "shot" glasses, lifting it to their lips and throwing their heads back so the alcohol could travel straight down their throats to their bellies with as little burning as possible.

"Lechayim! Lechayim!" they shouted in toasts of long life to little Esther and her parents.

From the very beginning Pinchas would hold his daughter in his arms and tell her stories of great Jewish heroes and sages like Moses, Deborah, Judah Maccabee, and, of course, Queen Esther. If you asked her father, he would tell you that Esther understood every word he said even when she was only one week old.

Malka would sit and cuddle Esther as she gave her warm milk in a bottle. *"Zai a mentsh,"* she would whisper. "Be a real good-hearted person."

As soon as Esther began to talk, Pinchas started teaching her verses from the Torah. Malka let her watch as she made the chalah for Shabbat. Esther played with the flour, tossing it up into the air and all over the floor. But Malka was patient, and soon Esther was handing her the eggs, one at a time, and the butter.

In Grodno, boys went to the school called *cheder*. Girls went only if there were no chores to do around the house. Because Pinchas and Malka had no other children, Esther had a lot of chores to do and no one to share them with.

Pinchas got up very early every morning to say his morning prayers. For the longest time, Esther got up early also and hid behind the stove and watched her papa pray. She loved the way he wrapped himself in his talit and rocked back and forth as he mumbled the words of prayer that sounded so secret and powerful to her. One day, the dust from the stove filled Esther's nose and she sneezed. Pinchas removed the talit from around his head and discovered his little daughter's hiding place. From that day on, Pinchas awakened Esther when he got up and taught her the words of the prayers.

When Esther was five, the Cossacks came again. As he had done five years before, Pinchas swept away the straw from the secret door and led his wife and daughter into the cellar. Just as Pinchas closed the door over his head, he heard voices coming from the room above.

"Pinchas, Malka, where are you? Where are you? The Cossacks are coming. You must hide. We all must hide. Where are you?"

"Malka," said Pinchas as he turned to face Malka. "It's Sarah. What is she doing here?"

"Pinchas, you must bring her down here with us," Malka said.

And Pinchas went upstairs and brought Sarah and her husband Reuven down into the cellar.

They all huddled together in the underground shelter. When everyone was settled and hushed, Pinchas closed his eyes and held up his hands to heaven.

"Ribono shel olam, Ruler of the universe, hear my prayer." And Pinchas prayed. Esther sat cross-legged on the dirt floor, with her head resting in her hands, watching her papa in wide-eyed wonder.

The Cossacks did not come to the home of Pinchas and Malka that night.

Years passed. Esther grew up to be a beautiful woman. She had learned how to sew and keep house, as all the girls in Grodno had learned.

"Our homes are our *shtiblach,"* Malka would tell her. "It is up to us to serve God here and make this a place God would come to visit. It is not easy to keep a good Jewish household. But you'll learn, you'll learn." And Esther did learn. But household management was not all she studied. Early in the mornings, before Malka got up, Esther and Pinchas prayed together and studied Torah together. It was their own little secret. No one knew about their studying, and no one would ever find out. Never!

When it was time to find a husband for Esther, Pinchas had no problems. Esther was beautiful and bright. Many young men wished to marry her, and Pinchas had many offers. Finally, he accepted the proposal of a young merchant named Avreml. Avreml came from a very wealthy and respected family in Kovno. He was as handsome as Esther was beautiful. He was even-tempered and a Torah scholar.

It was a match made in heaven!

People talked about their wedding for years. Everyone in Grodno and Kovno was in attendance. There were three *badchanim,* the wedding jesters, who told stories and jokes. There was a band and more food than all Poland could have eaten in a whole week: herring, and brisket, and breads, and *rugelach,* and *schnapps.* Of course, there was the special golden broth, a rich soup made from chicken and poured into a huge silver tureen placed on the head table in front of the bride and groom.

Esther and Avreml made their home in Kovno. It was hard for her to leave her family behind in Grodno. She had many memories of her life with her mama and papa. Most of all, she remembered those early morning sessions, praying and studying with Pinchas. Even though she had moved away from her father, she still got out of bed long before the sun came up to pray just like her papa did. When she covered her eyes with her hands, she dwelled in that silent darkness for a few moments and felt her father beside her.

About a year later, Esther was pregnant and expecting their first child very soon. Outside, she heard the thunder of galloping horses and the terrifying yelps of the Cossacks. Quickly, she and Avreml made their way to the door leading to a secret cellar. Carefully, they climbed down the ladder and closed the door behind them.

Would this be the night when the Cossacks raided Kovno and attacked their home?

Esther closed her eyes and lifted her hands to heaven. *"Ribono shel olam,* Ruler of the universe, hear my prayer." And Esther prayed.

The Cossacks did not come to the home of Esther and Avreml that night—but they were visited by someone else. There, in the midst of the pogrom, Esther gave birth to a son.

The verse from Deuteronomy is taken from one of the two songs in the Torah ascribed to Moses. The other song is found in Exodus

15:1–19 and, although credited to Moses, it is most often referred to as "The Song at the Sea." The song contained in *Ha'azinu* reviews Israel's history in terms of its relationship with God. While the earlier song celebrates the redemptive might of God that rescued Israel from the hands of Pharaoh and his armies, this song reminds the Israelites of the importance of their continued loyalty to God as they prepare to enter the Promised Land and begin a new era in their history. It instructs them to "remember the days of old" and the wonders that God performed for our ancestors in those times. Knowledge of those wonders is passed from one generation to the next. Tradition is that kind of intergenerational transmission. It insures that there is no weak nor missing link in the chain of our people. "Just Like Papa Did" illustrates how such transmission occurred in one family, releasing great redemptive power. Perhaps, it raises a question for us: Have we sought to pass anything of true redemptive power on to our children?

What kind of advice does our verse contain? Why would Moses want to tell it to the Israelites just before he was to die? What can we learn from our past? What did Esther learn from her father? What kind of power did this lesson have? What kinds of Jewish lessons have you learned from your parents or from your religious school teachers? Name some Jewish customs, ideas, or values you will want to pass on to your children?

· VEZOT HA-BERACHAH ·

> So Moses the servant of the Lord died there, in the land of Moab, at the command of the Lord. He buried him in the valley in the land of Moab, near Beth-peor; and no one knows his burial place to this day. . . . Never again did there arise in Israel a prophet like Moses—whom the Lord singled out, face to face.   Deuteronomy 34:5–6, 10

→)) ((←

God's Kiss

MOSES HAD BROUGHT THE ISRAELITES through the desert to Mount Nebo. From there they could see the Jordan River, and beyond it the land of Canaan. That was the land that God had promised first to Abraham, many years before, and then to Moses, and then to the Israelites themselves. And, finally, they had made it. Forty years of wandering in the desert. Forty years of wondering if they would ever see the Promised Land.

There at Mount Nebo God appeared to Moses. This was nothing new. Moses and God had spoken with each other many times before. Yet, this time God said to Moses, "Come and walk with Me." And Moses knew that there was something very different about this conversation, but he did not know what.

So Moses walked with God as only Adam had in the Garden of Eden, and Noah had in his generation, and Abraham had. It was special to "walk with God." As they walked, they spoke with one another.

"The land beyond the Jordan River is a beautiful land," said Moses. "The people have waited so many years to get here, and now they are anxious to cross over the Jordan and explore. They want to set up homes, real homes with roofs over their heads— places where they will stay for the rest of their lives. No more wandering. They have had enough of that. Now all they want is a chance to live off their land and raise their families in service to You."

"That is all I ask," responded God. "This is the land that I promised to you and to them. It will remain yours as long as you keep your promises to Me."

There was a long silence as God and Moses walked. They climbed part way up Mount Nebo to a place called Pisgah. From there Moses could see for miles into the Promised Land. Neither spoke for many moments. Finally, God whispered.

"Moses, I have shown you the view from here because I wanted you to see this land. It was you who led My people here. But the time has come for you to die, and you will not get to enter the land."

These words went through Moses like a knife. He felt a sharp pain in his chest. Never had he expected to hear these words. Feeling woozy and sick to his stomach, he reached for a rock on which to sit. God was aware of how much these words hurt Moses.

"It must happen to all creatures that they die. It happens to the ant and the grasshopper. It happens to the giant elephant and the powerful lion. All that live must die one day. Your day has now come."

"But, it can't be. Not yet. It's not fair," cried Moses. "I led the people out of Egypt. I led them for forty years as we wandered through the desert. I tended to them when they were sick. I gave them hope when they despaired. I brought them Your commandments and kept them faithful to You. Please, you must let me cross over the Jordan River and enter the land. Let me die there. Let me be buried there. If you truly love me, You would grant me this one last prayer."

God heard Moses' pleas. "Moses, I do truly love you. Did I not allow you to speak with me 'face to face' as I have allowed no other human being? Have I not sat with you during those long nights of doubt? Did I not choose you and you alone to give My Ten Commandments? Did I not give you My Torah and name it 'The Five Books of Moses'? I do love you."

But Moses was not consoled. "I have so much still to do," he argued. "Who will lead the people into the Promised Land?"

"We have chosen Joshua," replied God.

"How will the people know how to serve You without my leadership?" asked Moses.

"We have given them the Torah and all its teachings," said God softly.

"When they become frustrated and full of doubts to whom will they turn if I am not there?" Moses persisted.

"They will have to find the strength that dwells inside them. They will have to discover how to stand on their own feet and fight their own battles. That is part of growing up, and now it is time for our people to grow up," God responded.

Silence.

"Will they forget me?" asked Moses.

"They shall never forget you," answered God. "Your name will always evoke respect. Never again will there be another prophet like you, with whom I spoke 'face to face.' The rabbis to come will call you *Moshe Rabbenu,* 'Moses, our teacher.' The Torah will always bear your name. No, Moses, your people will never forget you."

"How much time do I have left?" asked Moses.

"Just a few hours," said God.

Moses turned and left the mountain. He spent the rest of the day in his tent. There he made copies of the Torah. Thirteen copies in all. One went to each of the twelve tribes so that wherever there would be Jews there would be a Torah. The last copy he placed inside the Holy Ark, so that Israel would learn that the ark is where the Torah belonged.

When his last moments arrived, Moses gathered all the people to say *shalom.* He blessed them all and gave a special blessing to Joshua. Then he turned and disappeared into the heights of Mount Nebo. When he came to a place from which he could see the Promised Land, he lay down and closed his eyes. He felt a great sense of peace and comfort come over him. He was completely happy.

God came to him this one last time and kissed his soul. With that Moses died. Yet, God performed one final act of love for Moses. There among the rocks of Nebo, God buried Moses' body and blessed it.

Many Israelites tried to follow Moses up the mountain. For days they searched in vain. They never did find him nor his grave. To this day no one has.

(Adapted from the Midrash)

"God's Kiss" is spun from our midrashic lore. The rabbis put themselves in Moses' place and imagined what it must have been like to learn that he was to die—never to set foot on the soil of the Promised Land. The questions Moses asks were the questions that arose in the souls of our rabbis who raised them in his name. They are the same questions we continue to ask when confronted with our own mortality or that of those we love: But there is so much left to do. Who will take care of my family? Who will hold the family together? Will I be forgotten? Just as Moses was assured that his impact would be imprinted on the hearts of his brethren forever, we can be sure that the best of our lives have taken seed within those we loved who so love us. Those seeds grow, nurtured by the warmth of our memories. As Hannah Senesh wrote: "There are stars whose light reaches the earth only after they themselves have disintegrated and are no more. And there are men whose scintillating memory lights the world after they have passed from it."

What does the title of the story mean? Why did God give Moses a kiss? What did that mean? What kinds of things worried Moses? Have we ever forgotten Moses? What are some of the ways we Jews make sure that those who have died are never forgotten? Can you think of other ways to honor the memories of those who have died?